For everyone worn out by prescriptions to
"pray harder" and longing for a lighter load—including me

Praise for *All Who Are Weary:*
Easing the Burden on the Walk with Mental Illness

"What a pastoral, kind, and true book. Emmy is a trustworthy guide, a gentle prophet, and a fellow sojourner for the weary and the wounded. In so many ways, this book will lovingly shepherd the lambs."
—Sarah Bessey, author of *New York Times* bestseller *A Rhythm of Prayer* and *Miracles and Other Reasonable Things*

"When faced with the topic of mental health, Emmy Kegler offers something that is sadly rare from a Christian pastor: companionship. Not the trite 'I'll pray for you' variety, although she certainly offers prayer, but the rich and deep kind. The kind that pulls up a chair and says, 'I struggle with this too, let's talk.' *All Who Are Weary* is a refreshing change of pace."
—Matthias Roberts, psychotherapist
and author of *Beyond Shame*

"*All Who Are Weary* is a beautifully and gently written companion to those who journey with mental illness and a guide to help us all love one another better. No matter who you are or where you are on the journey, I hope you'll get this book and allow Emmy Kegler's powerful words to come alongside you."
—Kaitlin Curtice, author of *Native: Identity,*
Belonging & Rediscovering God

"*All Who Are Weary* is an excellent contribution to the project of changing that culture, getting honest about the realities many of us live with, and letting others know they are not alone."
—Emily Joy Allison, author of *#ChurchToo: How Purity*
Culture Upholds Abuse and How to Find Healing

ALL WHO ARE WEARY

EASING THE BURDEN ON THE WALK WITH MENTAL ILLNESS

EMMY KEGLER

Broadleaf Books
Minneapolis

ALL WHO ARE WEARY
Easing the Burden on the Walk with Mental Illness

Cover image: AdobeStock
Cover design: Cindy Laun

Print ISBN: 978-1-5064-6780-1
eBook ISBN: 978-1-5064-6781-8

CONTENTS

FOREWORD

Hello, Weary One.

A therapist once told me that all humans share the need to be seen, heard, and known—that under all of our facades, all of our behaviors represent the pursuit of at least one of those same three needs. But how do we make ourselves seen, heard, and known in a world that venerates strength and personal responsibility and "good vibes only" and faith systems that have denied our pain, have positioned it as an affront to God rather than the proof of our humanity?

I am a weary one myself; four or more of the following chapters were written personally for and about me, or at least that's how it felt. That's how it always feels to suffer, isn't it? That whatever we are going through is a personal short-coming, devoid of any larger sociological context. That we are simply missing a step, that our struggle or diagnosis or trauma is due to our own ineptitude. It's hard not to feel like this is what sets us apart from the rest of the high-functioning world, a world that appears to be undeterred, indefatigable, and just out of reach.

The truth is that all *are* weary in ways that are often invisible to one another. Some of us slip in and out of the world of the weary, and some of us have permanent addresses here.

No matter how long our stay, we realize when we cross that threshold that our common instinct is to hide our pain or brush it off, to make our suffering more palatable for the people around us, watering it down with justifications and minimizations. When they ask, "How are you?" we hesitate, running through the socially acceptable responses and coming back with "fine" when we are anything but.

It's not easier to watch the people you love suffer; like living out those dreams where you can't run fast enough, can't pull them out of the river that is sweeping them away, the helplessness is overwhelming. We rush to fix, to identify the problem and repair it. We offer up all of the tools we have: prayer, a listening ear, advice, suggestions for the things they may not have thought of. We want so badly for the answer to be an action, a box we can tick off. After all, if we can't fix their depression, their addiction, their eating disorder, what is it we *can* do?

Here, Emmy invites us into a world where the weary are seen, heard, and known, and those who love them are invited into the humble and clumsy work of witnessing, of being with the pain of others without reaching for your favorite fix.

Welcome to the not-so-secret society of the weary, and those who love them. Here, you are seen, heard, known, and worthy.

—Nora McInerny, host of the *Terrible, Thanks for Asking* podcast and author of *No Happy Endings*, *It's Okay to Laugh*, and *The Hot Young Widows Club*

PREFACE

I want to start this book with two confessions.

First: I, in the most official of senses, do not know what I am doing. I do not have a license to practice medicine, to prescribe medication, or to provide therapy. I have not earned a PhD studying some dimension of the relationship between mental illness and the Christian faith. I cannot tell you, dear reader, what specifically has gone wrong in your life (or in the life of a loved one, a parishioner, or a client) that has caused the myriad symptoms that can be categorized as "mental illness." I do not offer any of the words in this book to provide a diagnosis or a treatment plan from a qualified professional.

Nor am I, by conventional definitions, mentally well. I have been living with depression since my early teens. It's possible it started as early as age ten, which is when I went from a happy kid who loved to dance and joyfully made new friends, to the preteen who wrote a poem about her favorite color: "Gray is rain, pouring down." Something went wrong somewhere in there. We know that by twelve I had effectively self-isolated to the point that I had no friends; by fourteen, I was on my first selective serotonin reuptake inhibitor, which is the scientific term for antidepressant and antianxiety medications that help a brain correctly absorb the positive chemicals it is already producing but somehow failing to process correctly. I would bounce in and out of therapy and on and off meds for the next twelve years, until I also developed an acute case of social anxiety to the point that I couldn't grocery shop. I had to have my partner buy milk because the idea of driving to the store, getting out of my car, walking inside, and performing the menial tasks of selecting and purchasing groceries caused me to start hyperventilating, even as I told myself over and over, "Nothing is wrong! Nothing is wrong! You are fine!" Today I'm on an excellent regimen of thirty milligrams of citalopram, plus regular exercise, natural sunshine, and meditation. Most of the time this works.

But I want to note that thirty milligrams is the highest dose of medication I've taken in my twenty-one years of SSRIs. This book has been less "written" and more sporadically wrenched from my heart, like it might be via a battlefield surgeon equipped with only a crowbar. It was also written almost entirely in the second half of 2020, a time when the world, the country, and my own family was in as much isolation as our work and grocery needs allowed.

So, beloved, if you have come because your life is affected by mental illness (in yourself or in someone you care for) and you hope that over the course of this book I will be able to draw you a perfectly plotted map of your own easy trek to mental health, I am so very sorry. If I had those words, or if I thought anyone else had them, I solemnly promise I would offer them here. If I had the magic words to make a loved one stop drinking, to make the intrusive thoughts leave you, to help your church member or client unlock the bonds of trauma and leap away free, I promise that I would not only write them, but I would also distribute them free of charge in every corner of the world that I could find.

At this moment, I do not know if such words exist. In my life and in this book, I will testify that there are people who have found such prayers, or such confessions, or such mantras. Some people have found significant or total liberation from mental illness through the interventions of religious faith alone. But not everyone has found such freedom. What works for one does not consistently (or even often) work perfectly for another. In truth, what the church has too long prescribed for mental illness—more diligent prayer, more attendance at worship, more dwelling in Scripture—can actually exacerbate that same mental illness and its symptoms rather than relieve them. What we have thought was helping was often, in my experience, deeply harmful.

What I will offer is only this: my experience. I have served as the solo pastor of a small neighborhood Lutheran church for five and a half years. I have also walked this world with depression for twenty-two years, compounded with social anxiety for the past thirteen. Neither my mental illness nor my ordained ministry qualify me to speak as a professional; I am writing instead as a pastor and as a fellow patient. I cannot offer the magic words that have healed me or others; what I can offer, however, is the sketches of a wide and wandering map in which I and many others who live with mental illness of all shades are walking.

I cannot tell you what your path to greater wholeness (for yourself or someone you care for) will look like. But I can tell you that the Christian church, by and large, has misunderstood and mistreated mental illness. I can tell you that our burdens have been made even heavier by often well-meaning words. If you have come to yet another Christian book on mental illness with trepidation and shame and distrust, I can tell you: We're on the same page. I'm tired, too. Tired of what my mind does, tired of how my body reacts, tired of how the church and the culture around us interpret the troubles of my heart. I want this book to be a place where we rest together, where no matter what symptoms and diagnoses and experiences led us to this place, we all find a way to sit down and breathe deeply—maybe for the first time in a long time. What I pray this book provides, even in a small way, is a better religious and spiritual prescription for understanding mental illness within a biblical, theological, and Christian context, so that our faith might not be a compounding factor in our shame or a hindrance to healing, but rather one of the many components that can lead us to the abundant life that Jesus promises.

This is my second confession: I do not know what I am doing, but I trust that Jesus does. One of the most important lessons, in Christian life and especially in Christian leadership, is that none of us is Jesus. Not only am I not Jesus, but neither, dear reader, are you. And yet we often expect that of ourselves. Those of us who live with mental illness often berate ourselves, privately or publicly, for our inability to heal ourselves, to think or medicate or run our way to health. Those of us who care for people with mental illness may find ourselves awake late into the night wondering how we can sculpt the next conversation, what the perfect phrase is to unlock the pain and send our friend or church member or client into the world with a permanently renewed sense of purpose and hope.

So many of us, on any side of the mental illness journey, pour ourselves out for the other, exhausting our energies because we fear we are the only support for a person in deep distress and need. There are times when such compassionate love is liberating; there are many times when we find we have drained our little well of emotional capacity and caring into an ocean of unmitigated need. Mental illness is not a moment but a journey, and to walk it (or walk with someone in it) requires sustenance and endurance. None of us will succeed if we imagine we can, if we press ourselves hard enough, eke out the perfect words and touch that will bring a spirit back from where it feels dead.

I sometimes call Jesus the greatest cheater of them all; he could walk into a room and say, "Little girl, get up," and it was done.[1] He did not have to sit shiva with her parents, or deflect well-meaning Facebook posts about how "God needed another angel," or help a grieving family navigate the first Christmas without her. He just got to heal. I call this terribly unfair. In most cases of sickness and death—especially the death of hope, which is a driving force in mental illness—we are stuck with each other for the long haul. The journey of mental illness is a longer walk than the stroll to Jairus's house and back, and we are weary.

But it is into that weariness that Jesus speaks too. We might think, if we have failed to save ourselves or others, that we have failed altogether and we are alone. We might think Jesus has found a home elsewhere and left us to wander the long road alone. But remember, beloved: Jesus was a wanderer too. He knew isolation, exhaustion, frustration, and despair. None of those were a sign that he had failed; none of them were a marker that he was anything less than fully human, and too fully God. The long shadows of our own soul create no fear in the God who made the glorious darkness of the universe, or in the rabbi who wept at his friend's grave and in the garden of Gethsemane. Our suffering is no proof of our failure or of God's absence, only that the journey is not yet over.

I think Jesus knew this, and knows it still. I think Jesus, even at the moments when he saw the power go from him, knew that not all healing happens instantaneously, that not all of us will rise from our deathbeds renewed, that some of us will wrestle God for a blessing and come away with a new name and a bad hip. Perhaps he knew that for some—all?—of us, there would still be steps to take and burdens to carry. Perhaps he knew that we, like the Son of Man, might not find a safe place to lay our heads. Perhaps he knew, and so left a scattering of stones along the paths of despair and loneliness he walked, pointing toward the little creeks where we might find fresh water and the cave where we might scrape together enough leaves for a night's rest. The psalmist did not say, after all, *You deliver me forever from my enemies*, but rather, *You spread a table before me in their presence.*

The savior did not say, *Come to me, all who are faithful, all who are righteous, all who are true believers.* He did not say, *all who are productive*, or *all who are able-bodied*, or *all who fit neatly into society's expectations.* He did not say, *who have perfected their beliefs, achieved happiness, proven themselves worthy.* The savior did not say, *and I will give you wealth*, or *I will* give you health, or *I will give you secret knowledge that frees you from the trappings of being a human being in a human body.* He did not say, *take my yoke upon you or perish forever*, or *take my yoke upon you and suffer for the glory of the church.*

He said:

Come to me, all who are weary and heavy-laden, and I will give you rest. Take my yoke upon you, and learn from me, for I am gentle and humble of heart; my yoke is easy, and my burden is light. And when I am exhausted on my journey, when my heart and mind and body and soul cry out for respite from the fight they wage against themselves, I cling to that promise.

This book is not a guide to salvation, mine or yours. All I can offer here is a pastoral and patient-side experience of mental illness, some faithful and biblical wonderings about how to speak of it, and what questions we might ask ourselves or others to promote healing and lighten the load.

If you are here because you are weary, and nothing else has worked, and you are just about *done*:

Me too.

Let's walk together.

AUTHOR'S NOTE

There are a lot of words in this book.
Many of them might be words you've never heard
    from a Christian before.
Many of them are going to be words that get whispered,
or talked around, conversationally sidestepped.
You might be reading words here that you think you
    can't say,
because no one around you will say them.
Too often we're too careful
with how we step, word-wise,
as if mental illness is a linguistic minefield
but as long as we tiptoe around diagnoses and symptoms,
we'll never hit the explosion of dealing with reality.
But I believe in a God of truth,
and that means using words that mean what they mean.
Like:
depression.
medication.
paranoia.
suicide.
Because the truth is, much as we might like to dress it up
in aphorisms and metaphors,

mental illness is a slog.
There's no tiptoeing here.
There's no leaving the minefield behind
for someone else to suffer through.
We need to find where the pain is
and dig down deep
if we're going to go on all together.

There are a lot of words in this book,
but there is one I will not use.

This word is not a bad word.
It does not have four letters.
It is not banned by the FCC.
You can say it in church (and probably you've heard
    it there).
This word is not fun to learn in another language
    so that you can whisper it in the back row of Span-
    ish II and giggle.

But what this word can do is make it feel like whatever
    is going on is going to last forever.
This word suggests that there are things that can't be
    changed.
This word can make it feel like healing isn't possible,
like recovery is out of reach,
like symptom reduction is just a lesser evil.
And this word can make it feel
like the first time is all you need,
like the first failure means you aren't worth a second try

like the unimaginable depth of the mind of the divine
is enough to keep all of us from drowning
in the waves of our own worry and fear.

This word used to live on the tip of my tongue in
arguments
and at the edge of my ear in sleepless nights.
Uprooting it has not been easy.
Sometimes it sneaks back in
like the tomato seeds in our compost pile,
sprouting sun-demanding shoots among my herbs.
It's not a bad word, in and of itself.
It just doesn't belong in my garden,
not this growing season.

I told you there are a lot of words in this book,
and I said there is one I will not use—
I lied.
(I will tell you when I lie.
I told you I serve a God of truth.)
This is a word I will use only once,
only where when planted it might grow
something that can feed all of us.
So here it is, but only once:
You are loved—
Always.

CHAPTER ONE

SIN

Crazy.

Insane.

Bonkers. Mad. Psycho. Wacko. Deranged. Loony. Cuckoo. Head case. Nuts.

There are plenty of words for people like me. It is a little ironic, or perhaps extraordinarily predictable, that we would have so many options for not saying "mental illness." Its diagnosis brings despair or dread; its mention, more often than not, brings shame or mockery.

We handle the disruptive behaviors associated with mental illness far better as annoyances and stereotypes. If someone annoys us with a rapid change in mood, we'll call them bipolar. Anything we invest a little more than average time or money in—crafting supplies, motorcycle upgrades, pumpkin spice lattes—is an addiction. Any situation that changes unpredictably more than twice? Schizo. I've heard many well-organized high school students refer to their color-coded notes as OCD.

All of these are a two-edged sword against those who suffer from mental illness. First, each of them is a misunderstanding of the symptoms of each diagnosis. One sudden change in mood is far less likely to be a symptom of a mental illness than it is to be the normal fluctuations of energy, stress, and hormones throughout any given human day. An addiction is not just an interest or a passion, but an intense focus on the emotional and/or chemical high provided by a substance or experience to the point that it disrupts the rest of a person's life. The wide category of schizophrenic and schizoaffective symptoms goes well beyond unpredictability into dangerous and destructive delusions, disrupted communication patterns, and excessive agitation. And obsessive-compulsive disorder may include particularly well-organized school supplies, but the behaviors will not be a cutesy love of sticky notes but an all-consuming and irrational fear that failing to perform particular rituals (careful arranging yes, but more often washing hands, checking the stove or lights or hair straightener, or hoarding any items regardless of actual usability) will endanger their lives or the lives of others. All of these are good enough reasons not to use diagnoses as punch lines, in the same way that we wouldn't joke that someone with a plaster cast must have a bondage kink—any actual meaning to the metaphor is so far stretched as to be ludicrous.

But secondly, and more painfully, to use either general terms for "insane" or slang for specific diagnoses is to make a mockery of the pain that mental illness causes. When we do so, often without intending to, we reinforce the idea that mental illness is something to be laughed at, or at worst is simply a minor inconvenience. We suggest, in quipping that "zomg I'm sooo crazy" that mental illness is just a quirky part of our personalities that makes for a fun Instagram story. The truth is that mental illness, for many of its sufferers, is a devastating and debilitating experience, isolating, shaming, destructive of relationships and livelihood, difficult to treat, and sometimes lifelong.

Even alternatives that are meant to avoid reinforcing mental illness as a mockable negative introduce new complications. *Wild, feral, savage*: these have long been applied to people whose mental illness symptoms caused them to act contrary to social expectations, and recently we've taken them back up again (especially *wild*) as an alternative to describing a political fiasco or a particularly out of control party as "crazy." This was, as so many things are, well intentioned, but in our easy swap of one word for another, we often forget what the new word's history might be. *Savage, wild*, and *feral* were all terms used for people of color, particularly those encountered by white colonizers or enslaved by white families. The alleged antisocial behavior of "savages" permitted their oppressors to insist that they were taking away their land, their bodily autonomy, their religion and culture, and their very lives "for their own protection."

The complicated language around mental illness is closely tied to its complicated history. The diagnosis and treatment of mental illness, now lifesaving for many (including myself), has had a questionable history at best. Distinguishing "unhealthy" thought patterns and behaviors can be a process of healing and self-actualization, or it can simply be a reiteration of toxic societal norms. "Hysteria," for example, has functioned as a broad category for any number of undesirable behaviors in women, ranging from epilepsy and dissociation to the truest mental illness of all, a woman who does not seek marriage. Under the category of "hysteria," women have been experimented on (all too often by male doctors), with treatments ranging from hysterectomies to hypnotic reenactments of repressed childhood abuse. Sigmund Freud, the long-hailed "father of psychology," has come under serious scrutiny not only for the complete lack of the application of the scientific method to his process and theories, but also for how he interpreted the trauma and fears of his female clients as core human nature rather than the results of abuse and sickness in their families and society.

How we understand mental illness, and how to treat it, is a medical practice in flux. Yet, this does not indicate that our current standards of assessment and treatment are wrong. When the day comes that we have a cure for cancer that is quick, pain-free, and long-lasting, we will reject excisional biopsies, chemotherapy, and radiation as horrors of a bygone era—but now, they are the best we have, and in so many cases grant better and longer lives to those who undergo them. It is the same, in many ways, with mental illness. We do not yet have a straightforward path to diagnosis, treatment, and remission; we do, however, have methods through which we identify symptoms and address them with a multitude of options (medication, therapy, habit shifts) that can benefit, even save, the patient.

This is, of course, only observation from one side of the therapist's coffee table. I do not have a degree in psychology. I just have a degree of mental illness.

This is not something I'm supposed to say. Despite advocacy for decades, mental illness is still stigmatized and silenced. To admit to struggles in mental health takes a particular degree of vulnerability—whether we confess it to one other person in private confidence or to hundreds of people picking up a book. Revealing a life with mental illness requires either a lot of trust or a lot of exhaustion, or a combination of both. Some attempts at disclosure or advocacy become glamorized and performative—depictions of depression as a little gray cloud, for example, or a paper plate smiley mask over our actual face, when what depression actually looks like is dishes left in the sink so long they grow mold. I don't think Pfizer is shooting that commercial any time soon. Mental illness is not pretty.

And mental illness is especially not pretty for me. Not just because of the dishes thing—because I'm queer. My identity only got loosed from the Diagnostic and Statistical Manual of Mental Disorders, the textbook of symptoms and diagnoses used for identifying mental disorders, in 1973. (Evelyn Hooker laid foundational work for this in the 1950s when she used a double-blind study to empirically refute the generally accepted psychological belief that gay men were more maladjusted than straight men. She did this using the Rorschach test. Yeah, the one with the inkblots. As noted above, mental health is a moving field.) A good portion of mental health care providers have stayed caught up, but too many members of my queer family know the experience of dealing with a doctor or therapist who doesn't understand our sexualities, and treats them as pathological symptoms or as the causes of our distress. This isn't limited to people with degrees, of course; try any forum on the Internet where LGBTQIA+ people exist, and you'll find someone who claims that all of our other struggles will be solved by turning straight and/or cisgender. Somehow, the problem is not that I have a chemical imbalance in my brain caused by slow serotonin absorption; the problem is that I like women. Fix that, and the rest will right itself! (I'm not sure how, because nothing depresses me more than the idea of life without my wife, but some guy on TikTok said so, so you know it's true.)

The symptoms and experiences of my own life with mental illness is complexified by my faith. Belief is the favored Christian prescription for mental illness. Pills? Heck no, just prayer! Anxiety? Cast it on the Lord. Depression? Leave it at the foot of the cross. After all, miracles happen every day!

My friend Sarah once told a story of her father's anxiety disorder and stomach ulcers, and how a minister promised him that yes, God could really heal. Her dad went home and prayed, thinking if the anger and fear would stop running his life, then he'd really know God was real. And bam—healed. No more anxiety. The first time I heard Sarah tell this story I wanted to throw something across the room. I'd been asking for the same damned thing for a decade, and God was spectacularly silent. I do not remember a time when I could shop for clothes without ending up in a sweaty, feverish, flushed mess, panic-breathing in the dressing room, with my anxiety caterwauling like an invisible infant strapped to my chest, the panic alarm coming from both inside and out. The baby does not care that with every haggard breath I am asking Jesus to calm her down.

She is just going to scream, and I am going to once again go home without new jeans. Religious belief can be a beautiful release—and yet, if we take human experience seriously, we recognize that it is not a perfect preventative against mental illness.

Faith persists as a prescription for mental illness even when we have stepped back from offering it for physical ailments. We would be wary of someone who encouraged their diabetic parent to give up the medications and the diet changes and to cast their insulin needs on Christ alone. We take our kids to the doctor for a dislocated shoulder, we hand them over to a dentist and anesthetist to pull their incoming wisdom teeth, we post on Facebook every October to remind everyone to do self-exams and those over 45 to schedule their mammograms. Yet when it comes to a sickness in our hearts and minds, we whisper about Wellbutrin as if it's direct mailed from a witch in the woods; *don't let anyone find out.* We'll treat the pneumonia in our lungs and the cholesterol in our blood—we take medications, we change our diet, we go for walks—but we treat our brains as some kind of magical container for entirely controllable thoughts rather than an organ in a body dictated by all sorts of random and contextual events. Our brains are, essentially, fatty tissue, powered by ooze made of electricity and chemicals. Yet we act as if they have somehow transcended the bonds of mortality and can consistently make good choices as long as our faith is good enough. We recognize that even Jesus was fully human, given to despair and anger and probably a hammered thumb at least once,[1] but we fail to extend the same grace to ourselves.

Faith, as a "treatment" for mental illness, takes a multitude of "diagnostic" forms. In general, the church fails to specify exactly how and why faith will heal, only that it will. The moment we scratch the theological surface, we find a whole host of bad theology and bad psychology masquerading as "biblical truth."

Sometimes the church has approached mental illness as sin. Perhaps we are not mentally ill, but rather self-indulgent, self-oriented. It's a weird twisted sense of pride, that we who live with mental illness are so focused on our own wretchedness or our own isolation from others that we distort our relationship with God and with our neighbor. We are the pinnacle of *incurvatus in se*, of a human obsessed with itself. I believe categorizing mental illness as a sin is a fundamental misunderstanding of both. I do not enjoy my mental illness. There is nothing fun or glamorous about having to go home from the grocery store without milk because my anxiety screamed too loud for me to handle the checkout line. There is no self-indulgence there; there is only compounding shame. There are certainly circumstances in which I indulge a bad mood at the expense of the people around me, which is an *actual* sin. A panic attack in a parking lot is not that.

Sometimes the church has taught of mental illness as not the sin, but the *fruit* of sin. Perhaps, the church has wondered, if my faith were better, if I prayed more, if I believed more rightly, if I led a truly "biblical" life, then the symptom (mental illness) of my sin (the lack of faith) would lessen. I have the fortune of being a pastor, with the history and tools at hand to reject outright any belief that we can strengthen our own faith, since it is not our doing but entirely a gift of the Holy Spirit—but of course, this is a theological cop-out. The majority of the American church, including my fellow Lutherans, act as if we believe in some system of point-grubbing in which we can pull ourselves up by our own spiritual boot-straps. Blame it on rugged frontier individualism, resign it to a pervasive symptom of Calvinism, but at the end of the day, we really think we can do it ourselves, and any evidence to the contrary is just proof we didn't try hard enough.

Sometimes the church has interpreted mental illness as a part of discipleship. Perhaps, the church suggested, our suffering is our "cross to bear." In this understanding of mental illness, the suffering involved becomes sacrificial. We may be encouraged to "give it up for Jesus" or reminded of Paul's own thorn in his side. We are suffering for the kingdom. Suffering is a part of the Christian way, after all. Jesus called us to take up our cross and follow, and this mental illness is our particular cross to bear. My friend Jen and I have laughed, over very good whiskey, about this teaching. It is such a poor reading of God's work for us in Jesus's crucifixion that it almost seems like someone was *intending* to weaponize our symbol of salvation into an object of abuse. It teaches that suffering is redemptive only for suffering's sake. It has no interest in condemning those who put the savior of the world on the cross, or questioning the religious and political systems that execute without cause. The core tradition around the cross is that Jesus did it *for us.* It has purpose, it has benefits, it transforms us, it liberates us. I can tell you from twenty years of experience that my depression does none of this. It does not benefit or save or free me or anyone else.

Sometimes the church has proclaimed that mental illness is a test of faith. Perhaps, the church wonders, this is a way of seeing if my convictions can hold out through the darkest trials. Am I strong enough to still believe in Christ's saving work? Can I, like Paul, run the race to win it? Can I, like the many psalmists, maintain my conviction in God's goodness and mercy despite the waves of desolation that threaten to overwhelm me? Jesus commanded us not to worry, after all. Will I, like Job, be found faithful? In this, again, the problem comes back to me. It has nothing to do with my physical state, my mental patterns, my past experiences. If I just tried harder, I wouldn't be so broken.

Sometimes the church goes in an entirely different direction and declares the problem entirely out of my control. Perhaps, the church suggests, the root cause of mental illness is not a failure of faith in the patient, but a presence of another force entirely—a demonic one. This way of understanding mental illness is more frequently found among church leaders and Christians dealing with what are often considered more disruptive forms of mental illness—dissociative identity disorder, post-traumatic stress, schizophrenia, bipolar disorder—but it is also applied across the board to all mental illnesses. In this particular scenario, neither medical treatment nor the faith of the patient will be enough to end the illness. This will require the mediation of ministers trained and confident in their power to identify and exorcise demons. Exorcism may involve a number of physical treatments including but not limited to bodily restraint, sensory deprivation, sensory overload, starvation, and intentionally inflicted pain. The emotional, mental, and spiritual control wielded by those attempting the exorcism is difficult to overstate.

Treating mental illness as demonic possession may be particularly attractive to Christians because it bears the most resemblance to the work Jesus did. To our biblical knowledge,

Jesus did not encounter someone who had [...]sion, or generalized anxiety disorder, or di[...] he did, notably, encounter people who clai[...] demons—demons who, in some cases, could speak, [...] in other cases, inflicted bodily pain on those they possesse[...] People experiencing delusions and other separations from reality may describe themselves as being possessed, and even speak in voices of the possessing demons; some people who suffer from mental illness experience self-harm as a symptom. Could these be reasons to treat mental illness as a sign of demon possession?

The church stumbles when focusing on parallels between Jesus's encounters with those experiencing possession and mental illness today, rather than considering the whole of Jesus's healing work. Jesus heals, sometimes by casting out demons and sometimes simply with healing power, a whole host of physical disorders: leprosy, blindness, paralysis, epilepsy, the inability to speak. Yet rarely do churches prescribe exorcism to treat physical illness today. For the majority of churches that prescribe exorcism, it is for treatment not of the whole spectrum of sickness Jesus encountered, but only for those that are today primarily treated with medication—namely, epilepsy and mental illness. These churches endanger themselves and their people by prolonging the symptoms of mental illness out of a faulty—and unbiblical—belief.

I in no way want to deride the importance of prayer, especially communal prayer. The prayers that we offer up over our mental health, our depression, our anxiety, and the other illnesses that besiege our minds and spirits are as hopeful and as helpful as the prayers we offer over every other physical disease ι strikes us, from cancer to Alzheimer's to substance abuse. ιhe positivity makes a difference, sometimes even makes a miracle, but by and large in medical experience, the positivity can help but it cannot cure. The most effective treatment, to date, for the majority of mental illness appears to be a cocktail of chemical intervention, cognitive therapy, meditation, and/ or habit shifts (body engagement through exercise, nutritional changes, and so on). And yet, the church persists in prescribing only an increase of faith. We have relegated mental illness to categories of sin, or a test of faith, or demon possession; we have made it a weakness of the will that can be overcome by better personal devotion, or a cause for physical and emotional abuse in the name of "curing" it. We have compounded the shame of depression, addiction, or delusion through ignorance and isolation. What if the church taught that toxic positivity and denying medical attention to those in distress was a sin?

We have failed, too, to attend to how systems of oppression, subjugation, and dehumanization have been direct contributors to compounded mental illness in individuals, communities, and multiple generations. Women, people of color, LGBTQIA+ communities, disabled people, the poor—all experience specific kinds of mental illness at higher rates than their male, white, straight, able-bodied, financially stable counterparts. For a church commissioned by the apostle Paul to confess that "there is no longer male or female, slave or free, Jew or Gentile, but all are one in Christ," should we not reject systems of hierarchy and oppression that not only treat equal members of the body as unequal, but subject them to long-term illness because of it?

Women are more likely to be diagnosed with depression and anxiety, or conversely to have their symptoms written off as "that time of the month." And yet, personality disorders (such as bipolar disorder) and psychotic disorders (such as schizophrenia) are experienced at a near equal percentage between men and women. It would be unwise to relegate the inequity in rates of diagnosis of depression and anxiety to only biological or hormonal differences between men and women, especially in a society and culture that still treat women as second-class citizens. More than fifty years after the passing of the Equal Pay Act, across the board, women still earn less than men, even in equal roles. Women in male-female households still do more of the housework, even when both adults are working full time outside the home.[4] During the COVID-19 pandemic, American mothers in male-female households were three times as likely as men to take leave from work or quit their jobs entirely in order to provide at-home childcare.[5] Much as we might imagine ourselves to be liberated from archaic gender roles, the statistics and surveys show that women are expected not to share in an equal load of household duties, childcare, and out-of-home employment, but to excel at all three (without, of course, making more than the husband in the latter category). New medication trials rarely include women until latter stages. There is, to this day, not a car-crash test dummy modeled on women's bodies, much less a model that considers how airbags, seat belts, and other safety devices are complexified by a pregnant rider.[6] Compound this with the persistent de-vocationalization of women in the many Christian churches and denominations that deny them ordination and leadership, and we are faced with a demographic that is pressed on all sides. Should we wonder that any human under such stress does not experience anxiety and depression? What if the church taught that subjugation of one gender under another, to continued physical and economic and emotional trauma, was a sin?

The complexities of mental illness in communities of color are even more insidious. Black and Hispanic people are diagnosed with depression at a lower rate than non-Hispanic white Americans, but their depression is often more persistent.[7] Despite the lower rate of diagnoses, Black American adults are more likely than white American adults to report recurring symptoms of emotional distress: sadness, hopelessness, worthlessness, or that everything is an effort.[8] At least three factors contribute to this disparity in reporting. The generational and historical adversity of non-white people in America—from genocide, slavery, internment, sharecropping, and race-based exclusion from health, educational, social, and economic resources—undeniably plays a role, as mental illness continues to be perpetuated in communities with unhealed trauma. (The philosophy that trauma can be inherited has been largely based on the way that families pass down behaviors and expectations, but is lately being substantiated by a number of researchers finding different instances of trauma exposure passed to offspring transgenerationally through shifts in expression of DNA.[9]) In addition, historical adversity translates into socioeconomic disparity, which disenfranchises the people of color who experience it when attempting to access mental health care. (Lack of access to financial resources that would provide comprehensive health care also partly explains the prevalence of mental illness among, for example, disabled communities and nonbinary and transgender people, who statistically make less money and have significantly less job security than their able-bodied and cisgender counterparts.)

Second, perpetual marginalization of people of color through continuing racism and white supremacy, from overt to systemic to casual, compound mental illness. Non-white youth with behavioral health issues are more likely to enter the juvenile justice system than to be referred to specialty primary care, compared with white youth.[10] Native / Indigenous Americans are diagnosed with significantly higher rates of post-traumatic stress than any other racial or ethnic group.[11] Meanwhile, Asian American and Pacific Islander adults are, of all American racial groups, least likely to seek mental health services—three times less likely than their white counterparts.[12] A prevalence of mental illness seems almost a foregone conclusion, yet the majority of non-white racial and ethnic groups are diagnosed with mental illness and seek treatment at lower rates. Why would ethnic and racial minority groups—sent into the prison pipeline at younger ages and higher percentages than white youth, systematically passed over for jobs and careers, arrested at higher rates and charged with heavier sentences, stereotyped or forgotten in almost all consumer media—not experience a higher rate of mental illnesses?

The most powerful factor in reducing the experience of mental illness in people of color is not some racially based strength of soul but rather a compounding experience of external and internalized racism: *underdiagnosis*. Simply put, people of color are statistically less likely to seek mental health treatment, and doctors and psychiatrists are less likely to diagnose mental illness in them. For many people of color, mental illness is laughed off as a "white person's problem"—not something experienced only by white people, but rather something that people of color cannot afford, fiscally or culturally, to experience. Many people of color simply do not see their experiences as worthy of the diagnosis of mental illness. Historical and familial trauma, in fact, can compound this belief: "we survived [slavery, genocide, the Holocaust], how could I not survive this?" There is great strength, for oppressed communities, in individual and communal celebration for how far the world has progressed: "Have not our weary feet come to the place for which our fathers sighed?"[13] Extraordinary inspiration is drawn from the patience and determination of a people who have escaped twenty different kinds of slaughter. Yet that pride and hope can quickly be turned to internalized shame when individuals and communities feel not joy but despair—often, despair caused or compounded by the very obstacles that they are supposed to rejoice in overcoming. If the symptoms of mental illness are understood as a shameful personal failure rather than a consequence of existence and trauma, an individual is obviously less likely to seek treatment.

Additionally, the health care system in America has a long history of mistreating people of color as well as misunderstanding their symptoms of mental illness. In Black communities run the histories of Henrietta Lacks, the Tuskegee Syphilis Study, experimental gynecological surgeries performed on enslaved women without any type of anesthesia. The supposedly scientific-minded European colonizers, encountering native populations in the "New World," brought smallpox, measles, and flu—by some estimates, killing ninety percent of the Indigenous American population. This is not only a historical problem. Black men with symptoms of bipolar disorder are significantly more likely to be diagnosed with schizophrenia if the doctor is aware of their ethnicity;[14] Black teenagers are fifty percent more likely than white peers to display symptoms of bulimia, but are diagnosed with it significantly less, even when symptoms are identical.[15]

Providers of mental health care in the secular sector have long acknowledged all this: our ability to experience love and acceptance, or to pursue our passions and develop our talents, is seriously hindered when our physical needs and sense of safety and stability are unmet or endangered. Even though therapists and analysts recognized for decades that our physical security is a crucial part of developing greater personal resources for mental health and wellness, it is only recently that practitioners have begun engaging in and encouraging responsive practices. Within the mental health field, there was (and remains, in some places) significant competition between different systems of treatment: medication, talk therapy, Dialectical behavior therapy (DBT) group therapy, and so on. Only recently have practitioners across the board begun exploring what is commonly called "trauma-informed" care, a series of approaches that attempt to shift the treatment plan from beginning at "What are the symptoms that need changing?" to "What events and systems have caused these symptoms to form?" Within all that, of course, is the growing realization that clinical care is not accessible or affirming for many people across many scenarios: affordability and lack of insurance coverage, language barriers, schedule incompatibility with working or childcare hours, physically inaccessible offices, cultural or familial stigma.

Thus is the work of the secular mental health care field, at its best: a multitude of schools of thought and approaches to treatment, working in concert, with continued acknowledgment that much is still unknown and will need innovation and revision. In contrast, too often, the "Christian" approach has been to ignore the rotten fruits of its own isms and phobias, perpetuating systemic traumas against marginalized populations, shaming and demonizing individuals at any level who experience symptoms of mental illness, while insisting that its approach is perfectly historical, literally biblical, theologically sound, and solely salvific. Seeking care outside the borders of the church has been proof not of the church's failure to care for the least of these among them, but a failure of faith (and, often, an endangerment of salvation) on behalf of the patient.

The church's most common framework for mental illness has been to categorize it as a form of sin. The burden is then laid upon the sufferer to repent of their own failure of faith and to seek remediation for it through submission to God's will, usually through prayer and Bible study, which will be proven to be done correctly only through a remission of symptoms. Persistence of symptoms, of course, will be an indicator that the patient is not faithful enough, not devoted enough, not righteous enough.

We see the sickness in this, right?

Our brains can be affected by any multitude of factors from the chemicals in the ooze not absorbing properly to the sun going down an hour early. Our minds and hearts, on an emotional and mental level, are composites of what has happened to us (and to our parents and grandparents and our population subsets), with a good amount of thoughts, feelings, and behaviors becoming so habitual that only serious and direct intervention can steer them in a new way. On a communal level, we are social creatures who seek out connection with others, yet can be deeply wounded by instances of that same connection. Yet the church's stance toward mental illness—making it a burden for the patient themselves to unravel through proper "devotion"—rejects all these facts about ourselves.

The church's most common framework for mental illness has been to categorize it as a form of sin. What if, in fact, the church's desire to make mental illness a problem of the individual's faith, rather than to recognize it as a medical condition requiring treatment *and* as a potential symptom of a sick society—what if *that* is a sin?

QUESTIONS TO ASK

Each chapter of this book will offer questions to ask those walking with mental illness. These questions are intended to be helpful for family, friends, pastors, and therapists who work with those with religious experiences, and for those of us who live with mental illness.

- What first comes to mind when you hear the words "mental illness"?
- What is a core memory for when you learned about mental illness? *(You might have learned something in*

school, or had a friend or family member with a particular diagnosis, or experienced symptoms yourself and sought an explanation.)

- What messages have you received from the church (your own congregation or the wider Christian culture) about mental illness?
- When you think about mental illness and God, what do you most want to learn or experience?

FURTHER READING

On the historical development of "mental illness": Andrew Scull, *Madness in Civilization: A Cultural History of Insanity from the Bible to Freud, from the Madhouse to Modern Medicine*, Princeton University Press, 2016.

On deconstructing common Christian teachings on suffering and trauma: Rita Nakashima Brock and Rebecca Ann Parker, *Proverbs of Ashes: Violence, Redemptive Suffering, and the Search for What Saves Us*, Beacon Press, 2002.

On new frameworks for understanding mental illness within a Christian context: Marcia Webb, *Toward a Theology of Psychological Disorder*, Cascade Books, 2017.

CHAPTER TWO
PRAYER

"Justin Bieber hair" was a revelation.

We were on a confirmation retreat, with forty high schoolers from three different churches packed into two cabins with never enough chaperones for how late they wanted to stay up and get into mischief. We were out in the middle of nowhere, which I as a new Lutheran had only recently been taught was essential for the formation of faith in teenagers. It was also the middle of January, but as a lifelong Minnesotan, the idea of spending a long weekend in a deserted and frozen place with variable heat was not remotely new. I was just out of college and serving as a children's education associate at a local congregation, and as the staff member with the youngest back, I was tapped to go on the kinds of trips where the bunk bed mattresses were older than my parents' marriage.

As an only child whose closest-aged relatives lived nearly a thousand miles away, I was not accustomed to the constant tumult that an exhausted group of teenagers can wreck on the space around them. As a natural introvert who had only once gone to summer camp (to great disaster, and likely a story pride will never let me write) and who had an extremely understanding college roommate, I had also not had the chance to spend this many hours with this many people in almost no private space. (Some private spaces existed, to be sure, but they had already been taken over by fresh young couples and then disrupted by one of us meddling adults.) My confirmation experiences in the small Episcopal congregation of my childhood had been relatively short (an hour on a Wednesday night being the most our extracurricular schedules could permit). They were also difficult to navigate, as the class comprised four girls who enjoyed each other's company plus me, the serious one who wanted to know why we weren't spending more time reading devotions about our walk with Jesus. (Lord have mercy on the youth ministers who have had to lead me. If there are crowns for them in heaven, those years will mark a large diadem for each.) I was not at all prepared for the way that forty thirteen- to fifteen-year-olds smell after a weekend in snow gear, nor for just how random their minds could become if we did not give them enough outside time. The leaders of the two other church groups with mine were pastors, simultaneously energetic and wise in a way I tried to emulate and, out of inexperience if nothing else, failed. Suffice to say, I was not particularly enjoying the experience, and the sight of JUSTIN BIEBER HAIR broke me.

It was scrawled toward the edge of a long sheet of white butcher paper. We'd hung these makeshift banners across the full-length windows that looked out into the woods, serving both to diffuse the harsh winter light reflecting off the snow and to offer our charges a chance to reflect on questions we'd posed throughout the weekend. On one such sheet, markers of every color had filled in their answers: "Grandma," "ACT results," "world peace." Across the top I'd dutifully written, during one of our planning meetings: "What do you want to pray for?" And now, crowded along the edge, with a heart dotting the three I's, was JUSTIN BIEBER HAIR.

This was the era (2009, if you must know) when Justin's hair was long, trimmed just past his ears, with gloriously side-swept bangs. Anyone of any gender would have admired it, but we were a bit curious about how it got on the prayer list. The girl who'd written it owned up, collapsing into giggles as she did, and could not answer our questions of whether she was meaning to pray for protection over his coif or her own acquisition of it. We moved on—or at least, the other grown-ups did. I sat there, thumbing over the edge of a camp Bible because I'd forgotten to pack mine, feeling the despair of not only being out of my depth but now not even knowing what we were teaching. We'd asked them so much about prayer that they'd worn down from sincere petitions to desperately needing to lighten the mood with ludicrous answers. How do you re-center on an intimate connection to the God of the universe when JUSTIN BIEBER HAIR is hanging there right next to "Mom's breast cancer" and "college applications"?

My dismay wasn't about the flippancy of a teenager hopped up on too little sleep and too many chocolate chip pancakes. What I was realizing was the difficulty of undoing centuries of Christian cultural teachings around prayer—not just for youth but for any of us. What our giggling pray-er had absorbed in her fourteen years was prayer as a Christmas wish list: put everything you can on there, and hope for the best. Throw something little in to fill the stocking, just in case Santa (slash Dad slash God) can't get you the Xbox. Yes, a cure for cancer and world peace, but in reality God hasn't gotten around to those in the past two millennia, so maybe a little personal request would be small enough for the Holy Spirit to pull off. If you didn't get what you asked for—well, God had a good reason for saying no, surely. That's what the Instagram posts promise: when God says no, it's because He has something so much bigger planned! Just be patient and you'll find out what it is. This works when you're asking for Justin Bieber hair. Maybe God had you destined for a fishtail braid. But the promise of an open window when we're facing a door slammed on our prayer feels extraordinarily hollow when the prayer is "Please, Jesus, I don't want to feel this way anymore. I can't do this one more day."

Numerous studies have assessed the psychological effects of prayer practice, but are difficult to control in a way that scientific methods would require. One-on-one hour-long prayer sessions are connected to decreased depression and anxiety and increased optimism in small samples of individuals[1], but how would we control for the benefits of simply having another human being who, for regular periods, sat and listened to our concerns for an hour and practiced the gospel of presence with us in our pain? Religious affiliation has been associated with a decrease in suicidal behavior in depressed patients,[2] but is that a decrease in suicidal ideation or a fear of eternal damnation for the act? (It is also worth noting that in a study of over twenty thousand college students, those who identified as lesbian, gay, bisexual, or questioning and also indicated that religion was "somewhat" or "very" important to them were *more* likely to have experienced suicidal ideation and attempts, not less.[3])

Prayer also contains a wide variety of practices in their own cultural and individual contexts. Praying in tongues, for example, might be of deep consolation within a Pentecostal prayer service, but could be disruptive and isolating within less spontaneous worship like Rite II in the Episcopal church, or even terrifying for an individual experiencing it at home alone. The rhythm and repetition of the Catholic rosary might be re-centering for one faithful Catholic, and sleep-inducing for another just as faithful. The Serenity Prayer, with its challenge to "accept the things I cannot change," can be restorative for those struggling with addiction or devastating to those suffering under abuse they cannot escape. Taking time to recognize the variety of prayers, both scripted or spontaneous, and how they work for each individual is crucial in finding what kinds of prayer might be helpful for those with mental illness. If we prescribe prayer as preventative against mental illness, we cannot ignore the myriad complications: the existence of religious trauma, the brain's own capacity for self-regulation, the theological concept of prayer as a whole, the inherent shame for anyone who prays and receives no relief.

Prayer is neither the shopping list for everything we want nor a vending machine into which we feed our righteousness and receive our every need. Why, then, *should* we pray? What is prayer taking us toward, if it is no guarantee of result? I experience prayer as the terrifying opportunity to open myself to the

God who made the universe, who weeps over the sparrow that falls, who counts every hair on my head, whose heart breaks every minute for how long humanity, writ in the divine image, still resists the eternal call to love one another. I am neither too small to come before God nor too big to imagine all my wants are of importance. Prayer sends me to my knees in need of mercy and forgiveness, and lifts my head in joyous celebration. It cannot transform my weary mind in a twinkling, but it can begin the binding up of my broken heart, and so often that is more than enough.

Prayer offers us a chance for **confession**—for sincere self-reflection and honesty before God. In Scripture and in twelve-step programs, this is known as *humility*: witnessing myself without delusions of grandeur nor the shame of self-deprecation. Christians may remember the story of the religious man and the tax collector; the religious man praised himself and his good works, while the tax collector only kept his head down and cried out, "God, have mercy on me, a sinner!" *Those who humble themselves will be exalted*, Jesus concludes.[4] Too often we have turned this blessed humility into a requirement, especially for those already marginalized by society, church, or family. Self-respect for our own hard work, healthy boundaries, self-care, and asking uncomfortable questions: all of these have been shuffled into the category of "pride" for which we should be ashamed and should subject ourselves instead to self-denial and degradation. And yet this kind of humility too easily sows the seeds of self-hatred and grows the fruit of mental illness, where the reality of our own capacity for kindness and goodness (flawed even though it is!)

is made unreal, and our mind turns inward only to our own unchangeable unworthiness. I reject this false humility as a prop of power and as wholly unbiblical.

We are made in the image of God. The tax collector has reason to mourn his choices, yes. He is a *tax collector*, one of the common enemies in Jesus's parables. Yet in only another chapter, Jesus will meet a real-life tax collector, in the wee little man Zacchaeus. Jesus does not send him away as a sinner (though certainly the crowd expects it) but invites himself to dinner.[5] Our humility cannot come at the cost of recognizing ourselves, each of us, even the rottenest sinner of all, as worthy of Christ's presence at our kitchen table. If our humility only serves to make it impossible to come before God because of our own assuredness of our unworthiness, it is not an act of the Spirit but a violation of the image of God within us.

Of course, we need the balance of humility. In the unreality of mania or delusions, or in the mental dystopia created in any healthy mind by the addictive bursts of serotonin when our TikTok goes minutely viral, we need a reminder that we are not God. To come before God in prayer and humility, to recognize prayer as a space for confession, is to recognize that we are not in control of our world or even fully in charge of ourselves. We are not fully bad, and yet neither are we fully good, and some of what we cry out for in prayer is relief from the consequences of our or others' hurtful choices. Prayer can grant us the gift of a compassionate presence, who comes beside us, knowing all our good and all our bad, all our in-between and all our hesitations, all our good deeds done out of bad motivations and our bad deeds done with good intention. Prayer offers us someone who knows us, fully, even more than we know ourselves, and does not praise us in glory or turn away in disgust, but simply says: "Yes. What next?"

Being fully known by God permits me in prayer to enter into **clarity**. What have I truly come before God to ask, and why? If I have come asking God to take away my depression and anxiety, do I know what I am actually asking for? They have been my companions for decades now. My depression diagnosis is old enough to drink (though let it be noted that would be a very poor choice). How ready would I be, if I woke one morning without them? What would I lose if their tendrils were unwound from my mind? What would have to come in to replace them? Jesus once preached that an unclean spirit, cast out from the person it possessed, would wander the world and then declare, "I will return home." It finds, Jesus explained, the house "empty, swept, and put in order," and then brings seven new spirits even more evil than itself.[6] Jesus compared this empty house of a human to the evil generation of the religious leaders demanding a sign, but I have often wondered: How able are we to fill our lives when the hardest thing about us is gone? Is it not easier, at the first sign of trouble, to go back to our bad coping mechanisms, our long-fought addictions, our most self-condemning thoughts? Do I really know what I am asking for when I ask to lose what has given me great sympathy for others, great celebration of friends and relationships that have held me up? I say that I am willing to let it go, but have I even considered what a mentally healthy life would be for me?

This is not limited to prayers for myself. When I am speeding through my prayers for others, I keep my layers of self-protection wrapped close. I do not need to think about why I am asking. I will keep it to the short list of those most in need, rattling off the names of the sick and hastening through *Thy kingdom come thy will be done* before I can recognize how God might be calling me to be part of its arrival. Sometimes we pray because we cannot think of anything else to do, and sometimes we pray because we know what we can do, and will do anything we can to escape it. There is a tale attributed to Sufi teaching that a believer witnessed the suffering of the world and cried out: *"God, how can you be the source of love and yet do nothing to stop such evil?"* And God replied, *"I did do something. I made you."* It is a lovely story, and frankly, most days I want nothing to do with it. The well of need in humanity is great, and to prayerfully look into it too closely is to risk drowning. My depression too quickly latches on to the enormity of the task, and soon I am lost at sea with no way to get back. I need clarity, where I see not only with my heart but with the wide gaze of God, who does not expect me to be all to all, and yet calls me forth to be the little bit of good I can. It is easier, much easier, to pray for Justin Bieber hair than to be clear on what I truly need to pray for and where I need to be the answer to prayer.

But in confession and clarity, the better understanding of who I am and what the world cries out for leads me not first to action but to **surrender**. I come to recognize that my prayers, as heartfelt as I may think they are, are not immediate direction for God or for myself. I need to remain in this space, in the presence of the all-knowing source of Love, and recognize that what I have come asking for may not be God's will nor may it even be achievable. If I am praying for the alleviation of symptoms or the end of addiction in a friend not because I want their wholeness but because I am exhausted by the weight of walking alongside them, I need to sit and ask: What is it that love would do? Does love seek a temporary separation in order that our compassion and energy for compassionate presence might be restored? Does love draw deep into the well of courage and speak, even for the seventy-seventh time, a truth that calls my friend to better recognition of the hurt they are wielding on themselves? Does love say, "This is as far as I can walk with you, for it wounds me beyond my capacity to recover to watch you continue in your own resistance to recovery"? All of these, I have witnessed, are loving responses, but simply because one or another is done does not mean they are done in love. If I choose one out of resentment, it is not love. The vulnerability of prayer allows me to be honest about what I have come asking for, and what my motivations may be.

Of course, some days, it is going to be good enough to only act loving, and pray the feeling follows. The practice of prayer does not promise that I will arise from my kneeling surrounded in a holy glow of perfect righteousness. The best I hope for, most days, is to have moved the needle just one tick closer to something like love, or to have convinced myself to act like it for the next fifteen minutes and then withdraw from polite society until I am better restored.

When I am praying to enact control over another or over God, I am failing to surrender to the truth about the world. I do not run things here. I do not run this country, or my state, or my congregation. My symptoms and my negative coping mechanisms are not something I desire, when I am at my best, and yet they remain a part of me. There is precious little that I can control, or truly should, because my view (much as I will laughingly tell you I think I am always right) is limited by who and where I am. My prayers will be only a clanging cymbal if they are done out of self-righteousness and self-prioritization. Prayer requires me to recognize, again and again, that God is God and I am not.

At the same time, the surrender granted me in prayer is not self-enforced conformity to "the way things are." I do not pray so that I might accustom myself to the world around me, and shrug off any pain or injustice with "well, God is on the throne." The prayer Jesus left us with is not "Thy will is already being done and we should cease complaining." The kingdom of God is not here yet; there is evil still, fighting against love at every foothold it can find. Prayer is not meant to make me complicit. Prayer is meant to make me not the center. Sometimes the surrender of prayer will offer me a mirror, reflecting how my own actions have perpetuated my pain, and I am reminded to schedule the therapy appointment or return to the yoga mat. Sometimes the surrender of prayer provides instead a window, by which I can see how the world around us still enacts so much suffering. The world maintains some randomness, much as I wish that I could prove it did not. Some tectonic plates shift gently, and some send tsunamis. Some politicians take the mantle of their power as a gift to protect and provide for many, and others hammer it into armor to benefit only themselves.

When I pray for the alleviation of my symptoms, for the end of my depression and anxiety, sometimes the answer prayer provides is that I am living in a world that profits off my own self-hatred, that works me into exhaustion, that demands too much of me to be restored if I do not keep my boundaries. Sometimes medication and sunlight and cognitive behavioral therapy (CBT) can only go so far to unburden me. The surrender of prayer reminds me that God is God and I am not, but also that the kingdom is not yet here.

Yet prayer rarely leaves me in despair. Not "never"; there are times when I try to pray and find it ringing hollow. My mind spirals, my heart aches, my palms sweat. Sometimes prayer is simply the space in which I am free to weep. The psalmists knew this; they did not forever find their resolution, only their hope, and hope does not forever quench the thirst of despair. Sometimes what despair longs for is not a promise of the future but a presence in the here and now, and sometimes the only drink it can tolerate is tears. I do not consider myself a failure in this. Jesus wept, more than once, and the stories suggest he had a full vision of the glory to follow the pain. If Jesus can despair, even when he knows the fullness of what is to come, I see no reason I cannot weep in my own limitations.

But, prayer rarely leaves me there. Prayer is a sending, a commissioning, a gift of **courage**. When I allow myself the journey through my own self-understanding and re-centering, prayer offers me the wrappings to bind up my broken heart. In prayer God says to me, "Yes. What now?" In prayer, I seek a mystical companion in the divine force beyond my comprehension that created everything, and the Son of Man born flesh who knows what it is like to despair, to feel alone, to be abandoned. In prayer, I am seeking connection with the source of all love who, two thousand years ago, stared down the emptiest tunnel of isolation and despair, and said, "We can do this. I'll go first." God is not standing at the end of the valley of death, urging me on like a scared dog on a leash, telling me to pray harder and I'll make it through. God is beside me, saying, "I know it looks like we're stuck in this pit, but don't worry—I've been here before, and it's not the end."

Prayer, at least a good amount of the time, comes up hard against mental illness's lie of isolation. Prayer, when I allow myself to enter into it, often sends me out with a renewed sense of **connection**—not only to God, but to the many people around me in need. It is not a shaming, no divine tsk-tsk about how *others have it worse than you,* but rather *others hurt too. Can you help?* In twelve-step work, we often talk about how when we do not know the next right step for ourselves, we can help someone else. Acts of service may allow us to escape the confines of our own spinning minds. The break from my own cycling thoughts can provide space to re-think the situation that worries me, or simply provide space from it for an hour or two. Sometimes the worry is still there when I return, but prayer reminds me that I am not alone. The world is not mine alone to fix; the sick are not mine alone to tend; the shadows of my own foggy mind are not mine alone to stumble through. Love walks with me. Love is far, far bigger than I am. Love is working with a tender fierceness at every chink in the armor of evil, pushing back against greed and hate and sickness and death, in what may seem like random acts of good against the march of decay but are from the distance of time a twirling dance toward the coming of the kingdom. I am not alone. Prayer reminds me of all those working for good, whether they know it or not, and all those coming alongside me in kindness, whether they know it or not. Prayer grants me the gift to face reality, not because I am resigned to it, not because I have control over it, but because I am not alone in it.

One of the greatest lies of mental illness—be it a major depressive episode, or paranoia, or delusions—is the story that we are alone. No one else is feeling this way; no one else is experiencing what we are; no one can understand the struggles we face. Prayer kicks back against the lies, and says: *Not only are you **not** alone, but I will give you strength to find your place in the world again.* Prayer does not leave me kneeling in the presence of God by myself. Prayer sends me back into the world, saying: *Hope is not done with you yet.*

QUESTIONS TO ASK

- How do you pray? How do you feel about how you pray?
- Is there something you would like to change about how you pray? What would it be?
- In the last six months, when have you prayed and felt hope? (It's okay if the answer is "never.") How can you re-create (or create!) that experience?
- What are you really praying for?
- How do you envision the God to whom you are praying?
- How is your prayer life changing you?

FURTHER READING

On new ways of praying: Meta Herrick Carlson, *Ordinary Blessings: Prayers, Poems, and Meditations for Everyday Life*, Fortress Press, 2020.

Sarah Bessey (editor), *A Rhythm of Prayer: A Collection of Meditations for Renewal*, Convergent Books, 2021.

Cláudio Carvalhaes, *Liturgies from Below: Praying with People at the End of the World*, Abingdon Press, 2020.

On practicing our belovedness: Henri Nouwen, *Life of the Beloved: Spiritual Living in a Secular World*, Crossroad, 2014.

CHAPTER THREE

SEEKING
TREATMENT

What is it like to be alone?

Not just at home, in early morning, with the quiet dawn seeping in through the window blinds as children and partners and pets still sleep, a warm coffee cup for company and the quilt of sky stretching out overhead. Not just at work, with the store clear of customers and the hum of a too well-known soundtrack just above the skid of a box on a shelf as there are a few precious moments to restock and breathe; not just at the office, where the background din of cubicle chatter accompanies a burst of productive solo energy. Not even at night, when the shadows press in and dawn seems far away—for even then, dawn is still coming.

No, what is it like to be truly alone? Alone like the sole survivor in a cemetery of souls, alone without a way to count the days or weeks. Alone without a hand to hold or an arm slung across your shoulder or even the sight of someone else's feet just sitting with you. So alone that even your own cries start to sound less human and more wounded animal. Alone not from choice nor from restful quiet but from abandonment and isolation and fear. What is it like to be alone because everyone else has left you?

If we are alone long enough, we forget who we are. We can forget what it is like to feel tenderness, because all we have known is pain. We can forget how to hear a whisper, because inside us there are only howls.

And then, into that space, steps God. Nothing in us is worthy to stand before the Holy One; nothing in us can tolerate it. God's presence is only a promise of torment and destruction, of further descent into the void. "Leave me alone," we growl.

And God replies, "What is your name?"

The Gerasene demoniac, who we meet in three of the four gospels, was so ruled by an unclean spirit that he could no longer live in society. He was cast out to the graveyard, living among the tombs. His agony and anger were so great that no chain could hold him. His pain was so intense that even bruising himself with rocks did nothing to ease his despair. And when Jesus stepped from a small boat, still wet from the storm that had just been calmed, the man-who-felt-like-not-a-man rushed at him: "What are you going to do to me, Son of the Most High God?!"[1] A gentile community, for its own safety, had cast out one of their own, and left him among the dead and perhaps for dead, and now he was held by a new community, a legion of unclean spirits, possessed by so much that could not tolerate the presence of love and life.

The church has long drawn a connecting line between mental illness and demonic possession, with the resulting "prescription" of personal prayer or, in extreme cases, exorcism. It will surprise no one, I am sure, that I am not convinced of this particular cure. Exorcism has been used throughout Christian history as a method for treating what might be better termed mental illness or in many cases what are considered socially inappropriate or socially inconsistent behaviors. Exorcism as "treatment" in these cases has often led not to the healing and wholeness of the person who is suffering from mental illness, nor to healing for their family or their community, but rather to their destruction. Perhaps most notable in this history is the case of Anneliese Michel. Anneliese began experiencing temporal lobe epileptic seizures at age sixteen, soon followed by depression and auditory hallucinations. Five years of psychiatric medicines failed to ease her symptoms, and she and her parents became convinced that she was possessed by a demon. Under permission from their local bishop, two Catholic priests began performing exorcisms on Anneliese, and she and her parents ceased to consult with medical professionals. Anneliese slowly stopped eating and drinking, and after sixty-seven exorcism sessions over ten months, she died of malnutrition and dehydration.[2]

When exorcisms are performed on people experiencing epilepsy, psychosis, or self-harm, they do not consistently lead to the person's wholeness or to their restoration to the larger community. And yet, some exorcisms *do* take place in ways that people experience to be healing. How do we understand this? For some people—particularly within traditions that are non-white and non-Western—exorcisms are healing; they appear to have a positive effect in which the person then experiences a greater wholeness, a release from an internal or external force that was not them but had them under their control. It is unwise, especially for me as a white woman in the American Midwest, to deny this existence simply because it does not work for me. It is unwise to act as if the exorcisms that happen in a multitude of cultures, both within my country and around the world, do not "work," or are somehow only placebos, or are all by nature abusive. I will not make that claim. It is not my interest to tear down experiences—whether simple personal prayer or long-term, institutionally guided exorcism, or anywhere in between—that have been sustaining or salvific for other people and communities. It is simply to point out that they are not *consistently* a source or guarantee of healing and wholeness.

From a psychiatric standpoint, it is not terribly surprising that the one-size-fits-all prescription of religion fails to fully treat any of the possible diagnoses in the journey of mental health. We do not have a single medication that can do it, not even within one category of the DSM-V. For many of us who live with mental illness, we know the long-term experimentation that can be required to find the "right" medication that keeps our brain in better balance, and how exhausting and symptom-compounding that experience can be. We are trying to fix the very thing that keeps saying, "You are not fixable." Every time our doctor or psychiatrist suggests a change in medication, we face what can be months of weaning off the current medication, starting the lowest possible dose of a new option, wading through two to four weeks of the side effects, and only after a month or more experiencing actual mental improvement—all while, did I mention, still fighting the yet-uncured mental illness that interprets all of these steps not as a journey to feeling better but further proof we are without hope.

We have much greater grace for a broken ankle than we do for our faltering minds. We would not say to a foot, "You're doing it wrong! Heal faster!" if the bones had not knit themselves back together after only a week, and yet this is the message we often internalize when facing down a new pill bottle at the pharmacy. We internalize, too, that if prayer or right belief worked for someone else, it must work for us—neglecting any sense of our unique brain chemistry, personal experiences, and religious history. Someone whose anxiety would react better to Lexapro than to Prozac (even though both are SSRIs) might also react better or worse when applying religion to the problem. And yet, although we can recognize the variety needed in pharmaceuticals, we shame ourselves for how our faith might fail us.

One difficulty, of course, is that when Jesus met people who are described as "possessed" or "in need of exorcism" or "held by demons," he did not refute such interpretations. When Jesus met a blind man and the disciples asked him, "Who sinned, that this man was born blind?" Jesus did not reiterate that the blindness is a result of sin, but rather that it is to show the glory of God.[3] If, when encountering someone who was demonically possessed, Jesus had said something similar, we might have a better case for claiming that mental illness was not demonic possession. But unfortunately, this is not the record that we have. He does not say to the gathered disciples, "Oh, this is actually a case of epilepsy," or "Don't worry, the neurotransmitters are just misfiring." No, he addressed the demoniac. He performed the exorcism—in some cases, had conversations with the demons who possessed the individual. How could a faithful person then argue that epilepsy, hallucinations, and self-harm (which we see in several cases of demoniacs in the New Testament) are not simply evidence of demon possession, but rather are symptoms of a mental illness that can be treated with medication, therapy, and other secular interventions?

In American Christianity, we have recently seen an explosion of preachers and practitioners of what is collectively called the *prosperity gospel*. Prosperity gospel is the term applied to a whole group of beliefs within Christian culture that in some way convey that financial gain and physical well-being (also known as "wealth and health") are rewards from God as a direct consequence of correct belief, positive talk and thought about God, and giving to the church. This way of thinking is particularly distinct to American churches, although it certainly shows up in earlier expressions of the Christian church and we've exported it elsewhere around the world. Most academic reflection dates the prosperity gospel to the 1950s and to concepts of "positive thinking"—that the way we think can reshape our reality, in a way that our actions alone cannot. This way of thinking is not relegated to Christianity; think of *The Secret*, or life coaches who teach "attraction" or "manifestation": *If you put good energy into the universe, good energy will come back to you.*

In prosperity theology, God's "no" to my beggy prayers is not "I have greater plans for you" but rather "you are not ready to receive that blessing yet." The requirements for entry into mental health are varied: tithing to the church, evangelizing, volunteering, theological correction, thinking and speaking of God only with praise and without doubt or question. Here the lesson is that my persistent depression is not the negligence of an absent God nor an imbalance of my serotonin intake, but rather my own failure to correct my heart and mind. I think I understand the premise, but it feels like blaming an asthmatic for not taking in enough oxygen: *Just breathe deeper!* I would never deny that promises of blessings for the faithful and generous exist in Scripture, but I do not witness them as a reflection of the whole of biblical testimony.

Scripture tells a wide story of how faith is recognized. Job's faith is so great that he is rewarded with the destruction of his property and the slaughter of all his children; even when his faith is proven true and God appears in a whirlwind to shame those who state that bad things only happen to bad people, Job is given no explanation for the suffering God wrought on him.[4] The Israelites return from captivity in Babylon to rebuild their temple and city, but never achieve freedom and self-governance again. The psalmists cry out over and over of their suffering while the unrighteous prosper, with their laments met with not God's justice but only the consolation of hope in God only someday to be realized. Paul dies under house arrest in Rome. And Jesus, God-in-skin, the full embodiment of all the goodness that created the universe and everything in it, is found not among the wealthy but in solidarity with the poor, and proclaims not "Believe in me and you will be rich" but "Follow me and you too will die."[5] I remain skeptical, at least from a biblical perspective, that faith is the only cause and health and wealth the only possible effect.

I reject this not only on the premise of biblical witness, but on our lived experience. So many of us can tell stories of faithful people who prayed fervently for deliverance from physical pain or illness and did not receive it. If we could just pray our way to the end of financial stress or mental illness, why could we not do so for cancer? Why not for war, or white supremacy? Surely God is not too small to listen to the cries of faithful Black mothers across America, who fall to their knees nightly begging for their sons to come home safe. And yet I write this only a twenty-minute drive away from both spots where Philando Castile and George Floyd were murdered by police. Somehow, God's power became limited to acting like the United States Treasury and a local pharmacist instead of the liberator of the world, and somehow it has become the victim's task to set themselves free, rather than the oppressor's responsibility to end their violence against others.

And yet, I cannot deny how life-giving the prosperity gospel has been to some communities. The prosperity gospel and manifestation theories have taken root in many parts of American spirituality not simply limited to Christian religion, and definitely not limited to one particular political mindset or racial background. Many people, especially those systematically denied wealth and health by racist structures in our world and particularly in America, long for the sense of an otherworldly power that recognizes their suffering and seeks to bless those who remain faithful. Many have found hope and yes, even success, in the prosperity gospel or theories of attraction.

Many prosperity gospel preachers, for example, are Black Americans. The proclamation that *through our own work, we can overcome the obstacles in front of us has* been a nurturing and liberating one for descendants of enslaved people who exist in a system and a society still largely prejudiced against their existence. We face in America a continuing racial divide, no matter how much our children's storybooks might try to tell us that their struggle for civil rights is over. Within these systems that continue to oppress, exclude, and marginalize people who have not fit into the category of white (or straight, or male, or cisgender, or able-bodied), marginalized individuals and communities may find some flourishing of the prosperity gospel or manifestation thinking. Because, simply put, they are people in need of hope. It would be disheartening to the point of absolute resignation to exist in a racist, ableist, ageist, sexist society—one that still runs America—and not believe that there was some greater force at work to turn the tables on such violence and bring us, *all* of us, to greater flourishing.

Almost any political or social activist believes in some greater force to which we must be subject if we are to change for the better: progress, free market growth, personal responsibility, collective care. Each of them believes, though the linguistics differ, that through commitment to that greater force, we might overcome the sins that still plague our country and world. In pushing back against the teachings of the prosperity gospel and manifestation theories, we must also recognize that those have been systems that provided hope for people who were denied it in every other opportunity, and we should be very cautious in judging them for it. Rather, where I want to push back is where these systems say that they are the *only* way to health, wealth, and other forms of salvation, and when they put the *only* pressure on any failure to achieve such on the individual rather than taking into account systemic disenfranchisement and disempowerment. Where these fall short is in insisting that they are a sure path to healing and wholeness, and that people who fail to find such "successes" are simply dooming themselves by a failure of self-control and self-correction.

In attending to the causes and treatments for mental illness, both in secular therapies and in religious and spiritual understandings, we are called to pay attention to the cultural pressures that individuals and sociological groups experience. We cannot speak of mental health treatment for BIPOC without attending to racism. We cannot speak of mental health treatment for women without attending to the way that society disenfranchises them. We cannot speak of mental health treatment for the disabled community without recognizing issues of access. We cannot speak of mental health therapy for the LGBTQIA+ community without recognizing the history in which "therapy" has been used not to support and provide for our flourishing but rather to dehumanize, destroy, and kill us. And we cannot speak of mental health within the church without wrestling with the long history, up to and through the present day, of treating mental illness as individual spiritual failure.

I am convinced that when we treat mental illness as solely an individual's spiritual failure, we reject the work of Jesus. We reject Jesus's work as a healer, and we reject Jesus's work as God incarnate.

Jesus, in his short years of earthly travels, encountered people with a multitude of illnesses and diseases. His healings, when feasible,[6] ranged over a broad spectrum: blindness, muteness, deafness, paralysis, psychosis, seizures, leprosy, hemorrhaging, edema. We often neatly divide the demonstrations of Jesus's spiritual power over sickness into two contemporary categories of physical illness (which many Christians now treat, without any sense of spiritual failure, through medical and scientific intervention) and demonic possession or "unclean spirits" (which are generically treated as personal spiritual failures, periodically needing the intervention of a community and/or a powerful leader). Yet Jesus makes no such distinctions. He offers healing coupled with forgiveness, as if paralysis is as related to the binding of sin as it is to a deficiency in muscle strength and nerve connections.[7] In the healing of a woman unable to stand for eighteen years, Jesus specifically names her as "bound by Satan."[8] Blindness, deafness, and muteness are alternately treated with direct exorcism or with simple healing; he does not consistently cast out demons or unclean spirits in order to open eyes and ears.[9] Unclean spirits are not limited to those who speak in other voices; they are everywhere in Jesus's work of healing, and yet today, we treat paralysis, blindness, and seizure disorders with medicine, while those with psychosis or other mental illnesses are still relegated to treatment only by prayer.

In the separation of mental health into its own category of spiritual success or failure rather than physical illness, we too deny the core theology of God's incarnation in Jesus. We are instead perpetuating some modern form of gnostic heresy that says the mind and body can be neatly separated, the body treated with medicine and the mind treated with prayer. If the human body was so negligible—if what happens to our bodies, and how they react, was so unimportant—what would be the point of the redemption of flesh in God's complete incarnation? Jesus could then just have been a ghost, here to free only our minds from the foolishness of our thoughts. But the earliest testimonies of the life of Jesus of Nazareth, and the core tenets of Christianity for generations upon generations, is that God was known among us not only to liberate our minds and hearts and souls but our bodies too. God knew from the beginning that there was no splitting us neatly into categories of spirit and flesh, no matter how that binary might have worked for blessed Paul. We get hungry and make bad decisions; we are fearful of failure and so subjugate others to elevate ourselves. Our minds can no more be neatly cleaved from our bodies than our present sense of self from the history of everything that has happened in the days and months and years beforehand, even what we can't remember.

In the same way that Jesus's incarnation and his miracle healings were multifaceted, so too are the most successful treatments for mental illness. For each individual, and at different times in each of our journeys, the massive toolkit of psychological treatment is applied in different ways. One medication offers more side effects than symptom alleviation; another adds fifteen pounds and also makes each day, suddenly and shockingly, manageable. Talk therapy takes a number of forms, sometimes specifically tailored to particular traumas and diagnoses, other times simply an open space for exploring the tangled and wandering threads of thought. Group therapy is revelatory for some and excruciatingly boring for others. Couples' therapy saves some marriages and closes others. Mindfulness eases anxiety or amplifies it; exercise provides more energy or saps it; diet changes provide sustenance or aggravate existing stress. Secular treatment for mental illness is as diverse as the people who seek it. Just as a river spreads into creeks and streams to nourish a whole land, or a tree spreads its roots and branches to deliver sustenance to the fruit, treatments for mental illness cover a wide ground.

We blame ourselves, sometimes, for how slow or shuddering our process seems to be. Plenty of us give into the early psychiatric ways of thinking, that with the intervention of a day of Prozac we'll be just who we have longed to be, or after a few therapy sessions we'll have taken off for California to finally commit to that perfect relationship we kept avoiding. And sometimes, annoyingly enough, it works. We try a medication and it sticks, or we get a therapist who says that soul-searing phrase that turns us upside down for weeks, or we cut sugar out of our menu and have sudden clarity of sight about Life, the Universe, and Everything (and we annoy everyone else around us who just wants to eat a cookie). And other times—and for many of us who live with mental illness, most of the time—treatment is the start of a long journey of lightening our own burdens.

Both the Christian church and its leaders, as well as secular mental illness therapy practices, often treat mental illness as a category. Individuals are placed into this category when their thoughts and actions are considered anywhere in the realm of personally distressing, socially maladaptive, or individually or collectively dangerous. These same individuals can then be removed from the category once their behavior has been sufficiently adjusted as to consider them "healed" or "cured." In such a system, any recurrence of symptoms can be feared as a sign of failure (or condemnation!) rather than understood as a natural process in the journey of healing throughout life.

What might be more helpful, especially for those of us who live with long-term mental illness, is to recognize mental health as a wide spectrum on which many points of humanity may fall, whether once in a lifetime or over a long course. For some of us, it may not be possible to move from the place on the spectrum in which we find ourselves to the place of what would be called "mental health" or "mental wellness" immediately or quickly, but rather to continue the long work each day of moving the needle a little further toward what might be considered "wholeness."

In the same way, we should not think of treatments for mental illness—especially self-reflection, talk therapy, and self-care—as relegated only to those who experience mental illness. Too often, we treat the treatments for mental illness that improve our moods, emotions, and minds as if they were treatments for something unique and unusual. We too often act as if therapy is crisis management, calling it in like a paramedic rushing to a situation that is fast-moving and dangerous. What if instead, we treated mental therapy like physical therapy—beneficial to those who have been wounded, yes, but also healthy and life-sustaining for almost every human being. Stretches and body awareness promote greater flexibility and healing for those recovering from surgery or injury, but they also do so for those who are healthy as well. Common chronic illnesses like heart disease often benefit from a shift in diet, but we can also recognize that eating in a way that nurtures our bodies and minds is helpful for everyone. In the same way, regularly sitting down with a neutral third party to reflect on the assumptions and learned behaviors of our bodies and minds can support a general sense of well-being long before serious mental illness might arise. Regularly engaging in sustainable self-care techniques that refill our energies and emotional resources can benefit not just those who have been diagnosed with a particular type of mental illness, but the whole of humanity.

Isolation is fertile ground for the seeds of desperation, and yet both the Christian community and secular understandings of "mental illness" act as if isolation is a key part of treatment. We don't know how to talk about mental illness, much less how to talk to someone going through it, and so we say nothing at all. Maladaptive coping mechanisms, behavior patterns, thought processes, and outward actions can catch us off guard, and we struggle to know how to re-establish a relationship that has been fractured by the symptoms of mental illness. Psychosis or reactive anger can frighten us, sometimes legitimately, and we often do not know what to do except to step back and stay away.

Or, we might fall into the opposite ditch, where in our desire to compassionately care for a person we love, we allow toxic patterns of mental illness to not only persist but to begin to invade our own lives. We permit abusive behavior because "they can't help it." We stay up long hours trying to logic through the illogic of an unwell mental cycle. We take every phone call. We become like Laura Linney's character in *Love Actually*, heroically there for her ill brother at every moment's notice, but then unable to experience anything more than fleeting joy in her own life. Women in particular are socialized to play these roles, for all other genders but especially for men who choose instead of therapy to have their mothers, girlfriends, wives, daughters do the brunt of emotional labor for them.

Neither complete isolation nor utter devotion are cures for mental illness. As those of us who live with mental illness work toward wholeness through multiple dimensions of treatment, we will need an intentional community that walks the journey of unconditional love with compassionate boundaries. The church is not the only place where such a community can happen (and often is not), but it can be one source of such. Perhaps the reason the church often relegates mental illness to an individual's personal spiritual failing rather than a call for community activism is because the church does not have healthy systems for long-term community care. We can pray; we can long for healing and miracles, but it is hard to walk the journey of mental illness with someone. It is hard to walk the journey of any physical illness, but in particular when mental illness causes someone to act out in ways that are draining on or even damaging to others, we struggle to draw boundaries in a way that recognizes their belovedness while protecting the community as a whole.

When we fail to understand how to effectively care for and treat someone who is experiencing mental illness, especially by making sure that they have support systems and that they are utilizing them, we relegate them to the same kind of exile as was experienced by the Gerasene demoniac. His demonic possession was so great that his strength caused him to break chains; his anger toward himself caused him to damage and hurt himself; he had been cast out from his community and forced to live among the dead, forced to dwell in a graveyard. He was alive, but his sense of self was on the brink of death, and for community protection he had been isolated. In healing him, Jesus does not leave him where he was, but restores him to the community in which, for everyone's safety, he could not previously belong.

The depiction of the Gerasene demoniac is a lonely one, and yet I wonder: How long had he been among the graves? How did he survive? Perhaps the community was doing as much as they could for him. They put him into a place where he would have little access to weapons. Perhaps there were women who snuck to the graveyard each morning to leave loaves of freshly baked bread, freshly caught fish, something to sustain him. We do not know. But the Christian church too often treats those of us who experience mental illness and who cannot be miraculously healed in an instant as Gerasene demoniacs who are fit only to live half dead. Our inability to compassionately provide care or to know when we have to draw boundaries is what causes even greater isolation and separation for those experiencing mental illness. When the church does not know how to care for those with mental illness—how to continue to love, how to encourage secular treatment, how to embody patience with the process—and therefore shuts us out, it is easy to believe the lie that mental illness tells us: We are alone, and we are unwanted. When we do not know how to draw boundaries, those of us living with mental illness begin to believe a lie just as damaging: Whatever we want to do, even if it hurts or violates others, is still permissible and fine and acceptable, because it's their duty to suffer for us.

The church, of all places, might be best equipped theologically to understand the journey of treating mental illness.

We know that transformation does not happen in an instant, that forgiveness and amends are a process, and that change is not comfortable. Medication, lifestyle changes, therapy: None of this is fun. Certainly we need treatment practices that understand our wounds and scars, and treat them with tenderness, but at its best, recovery from mental illness feels less like frolicking through sunlit prairie and more like Eustace Clarence Scrubb in dragon form. Eustace, nasty cousin to the Pevensie children of Narnia in a sequel to *The Lion, The Witch, and the Wardrobe*, travels through a portrait with Edmund and Lucy to join them on the Dawn Treader, a sailing ship headed for the farthest reaches of the sea. Eustace's generally grating personality reaches its pinnacle when, so greedy for gold that he falls asleep on a dead dragon's hoard, he finds the next morning he has turned into a dragon himself. Isolated from friends and family by his new form and his inability to communicate, sorrowful at his own pride and self-orientation, Eustace struggles with his tragic fate—until one dark night he is met by a huge lion. The lion, inexplicably, terrifies dragon-Eustace, even more so when he begins peeling the dragon's skin with claws that cut "so deep I thought it had gone right into my heart." But in that horrible, heart-searing peeling, the lion—Aslan, of course, though Eustace does not yet know him—returns the penitent dragon to his human self.[10]

Treatment, at its best, looks like this slow and agonizing peeling—and the church has, in its founder and its theory, all the tools to accompany us in it. Annual Lenten practices of self-reflection and repentance and renewal can mirror and transform the work of therapy, where we come to terms with who we are and what has been done to us and practice—often stumbling at first, but slowly becoming more adept—thoughts and behaviors that better embody who God invites us to be. The Christian practice of confession, whether it be in a private booth with a priest or a shared and public litany at the beginning of worship, reminds us of the need for forgiveness and the guarantee of grace. The long discipleship of following Christ in community, where our own beliefs and actions will butt up against others', can discomfort us in ways that while at first frustrating can become a path of great sustenance. Jesus had the capacity to heal in a moment; the church, and the work of the Spirit, has the gift of walking with us along as many moments as will be needed on the journey toward a lighter burden.

QUESTIONS TO ASK

Seeking treatment, especially when it isn't specifically Christian branded, can feel daunting for those of us with mental illness. Here are some open-ended questions that might be helpful to ask.

- What are you afraid of about trying to get (treatment, medication, therapy, etc.)?
- Are there barriers to access (money, time, etc.)?
- What solo activities help you feel more grounded?
- What group activities help you feel more grounded?
- When do you feel connected to others? What kind of treatment might help with that?
- What would feeling "better" look like for you?
- How do you think God wants you to get "better"?

FURTHER READING

On the gifts and burdens of the prosperity gospel: Kate Bowler, *Blessed: A History of the American Prosperity Gospel*, Oxford University Press, 2018, and Kate Bowler, *Everything Happens For A Reason: And Other Lies I've Loved*, Random House, 2019.

On healing, or lack thereof: Sarah Bessey, *Miracles and Other Reasonable Things: A Story of Unlearning and Relearning God*, Howard Books, 2019.

On the healing miracles of Jesus: Bethany McKinney Fox, *Disability and the Way of Jesus: Holistic Healing in the Gospels and the Church*, IVP, 2019.

CHAPTER FOUR
SADNESS

Do not grieve, for the joy of the Lord is your strength.—*Nehemiah 8:10*

I miss the days of believing it was that easy.

I miss the emotional release of being sixteen, with a newly minted driver's license and nothing to do that summer but community theater and Wednesday night youth group. After years of struggle and three different therapists, we'd landed on one that was close to home and also ran group therapy. I'd been on twenty milligrams of citalopram and a regular round of birth control pills for over a year. I'd made friends and kept them. Finally, I was feeling like my chains were gone. I was out of the pit.

Therapists began gently offering the word *depression* starting when I was fourteen, but the symptoms had been floating around in different forms since age ten or eleven. Something about me went beyond standard issue teenage moodiness—which is a whole debate in itself in the mental health community: What exactly constitutes mental health, in a bundle of hormones and identity crises? Whatever it was, I did not seem to have enough of it. My lows were lower, and harder to get out of. But now, now the ground was solid underneath my feet, and I felt like I belonged—including in church.

I loved Wednesday night youth worship at the Assembly of God church. Everyone was emotional. Everyone put their hands up and praised Jesus, everyone brought their Bibles and took sermon notes, everyone screamed with joy at the ice-breakers and wept with hands outstretched during the particularly slow music. I'd never seen someone cry in church before, except at a funeral. Now we all did.

My split with the Assembly of God would come over my sexuality, not over my mental health. However, I suspected that, just like my queerness, depression was not something I was supposed to talk about. Few there knew of my diagnoses and medications, though they were proud of me when I'd bring a friend from group therapy. It was only later, when the door had already closed behind me as I walked out for the last time, unwilling to be subjected to damnation for my sexual orientation, that I'd start to realize I was the only kid who cried *every* week. Not everyone wept during the altar call. Not everyone took desperate notes like the weekly sermon was the only rope ladder left out of the canyon of their thoughts. And no one else was bringing friends from group therapy. The joy of the Lord did not stick on me the way it did on others.

Sorrow and sadness are nothing new to life nor faith. They are not even unique to modern humanity; dogs howl when their owners leave, elephants mourn a fallen family member,

Neanderthals buried their dead in particular sites and marked the shallow graves with flowers. Grief over a loved one's death is a part of life; sadness over change and loss is expected. It is when this feeling does not fade in what is considered a "standard" amount of time, or causes significant disruption to a person's life, that it becomes an issue both of mental and spiritual health.

Sadness in the context of mental illness is most frequently associated with a diagnosis of depression. Here, the normal and human emotion of grief or loss has shifted into an extended period of feeling "down," with a loss of interest and enthusiasm even for activities that usually provided joy. Depression can be experienced as an extended period of symptoms that interfere with work or school, sleep patterns, eating habits, socialization, and generally enjoying life—but extended sadness does not necessarily equal depression, nor does depression only include extended sadness.

Extended sadness, or what is sometimes termed "depressed mood," can be only one component of mental illness in someone who is suffering. They might also experience periods of mania, or "elevated mood," as is found in bipolar disorder or in borderline personality disorder. Some people living with chronic depression experience periods of relative "normalcy," where they feel interest in activities and are able to engage with the world around them; it can be easy, when this happens, for them to feel that they are "better" or that they never even had depression at all. And depression in and of itself is startlingly common, for how little we are equipped to engage with it socially or theologically; an estimated 7 percent of adults in the United States, averaged across all genders, races, ages, and abilities, have had one major depressive episode (usually defined as lasting over two weeks) in any given past year.[1]

At the same time, "depression" is not a single experience of a depressed or down mood. It certainly includes prolonged or constant feelings of sadness, but can also be characterized by irrational irritability, difficulty concentrating or remembering events, sudden disinterest in passion projects or hobbies, unshakeable feelings of unwarranted guilt, a sense of personal worthlessness, changes in sleep (inability to sleep, *or* sleeping too much) or eating habits (eating too much, eating too little, or eating in random and indistinguishable patterns), and thoughts about death or suicide. Depression can also cause physical symptoms that cannot be attributed to other causes, like fatigue, headaches, and body aches. Mental illness, like any physical illness, is not "all in your head"; depression can be experienced as a sincere desire to do work or hobbies but no energy to do so. Depression, like all mental illness, is a physical experience. The brain, like any other part of our body, is an organ, and like any other part of the body, it can get sick.

Of course, Christian culture has not necessarily risen to the occasion in understanding or addressing depressed moods and extended sadness. There is an expected period for grief over death or loss, and once sadness extends beyond it, we lose religious language around it. "Weeping may last for the night," the psalmist promised, "but joy comes in the morning!"[2] Little comfort for those of us who wake on day two, or day fifteen, or day 365 to find that we are still inexplicably empty, sad, exhausted, and frustrated. Those who have not known a walk with depression or its sister illnesses can feel stymied and out of patience with those of us who might have everything we could ever need and yet cannot find joy in the world around us.

In some cases, there might not be joy to find in our immediate experience. Many of us who walk with depression do so not only as a result of a chemical malfunction in our minds, but as a direct result of our experiences and context. Some of us might experience depression as an extended period of grief; after a death of a close loved one, for example, we might grieve longer than is considered "normal" and find ourselves unable to find a way out of the feeling of loss. Children in particular who know significant loss—the death of a parent or sibling, or rejection either from one family member or the whole family unit—are more likely to experience depressive episodes. Trauma from physical or sexual violence has a direct correlation to an increased risk of depression, possibly not only on an emotional and behavioral level but down to shifts in brain chemistry as a result of high stress. Minority and marginalized groups that are individually or systematically deprived of the ability to fully flourish are also more prone to depression, and rates of depression improve when even some of those barriers are lifted.[3]

Years ago, I did a short chaplaincy rotation at an outpatient and residential treatment center for eating disorders. In a group therapy session, I watched a new counselor present the concept of "positive thinking." He passed out a worksheet with two columns, "Negative Self-Talk" and "Positive Thinking." The trick, he explained, was to shift from self-defeating statements like "I've never done it before" to "It's an opportunity to learn something new," and "I'm not going to get any better at this" to "I'll give it another try." The room (all women, as the treatment center had a 90 percent female inpatient population) was quiet as he walked us through each sentence, until he reached the end of the list.

"So, does anyone have any examples—"

"This doesn't work." A fifteen-year-old in a white sports tee with the sleeves cut off and the edges frayed held the paper sideways in one hand, giving him the ultimate *Adults are idiots* look.

He stopped speaking.

"Like, you get that this doesn't work, right? Like, that's nice for other people, but like, we can't just bam! think like that. Like maybe this works for, sorry, normal people?" She glanced at the group with an unspoken apology for the shorthand between *people without disordered eating* and *us*. "But like, we have a *problem*."

She wasn't wrong. Suggestions both within the church and within secular therapy treatments to change our thinking can work, but they require specific settings. Some of the disordered eating patients were so malnourished that the staff's only focus was refeeding—getting their body used to taking in calories again. There were no expectations for progress in CBT/DBT or group therapy for these patients, not yet. Their brains were so starved they were unlikely to make significant emotional or mental progress. Not everyone can change their thoughts.

Here is the secret we might not know how to tell you: Most of us do not want to feel this way. Most of us want to be as joyful as you wish we were. We want to get out of bed, to pick up our laundry, to do our work, to finish the project by the first deadline instead of the fourth extension.[4] Or at least, we want to want those things. But something in our body or in our immediate world is stopping us. We drop the bucket down the energy and emotion well, and it comes up dry. We know you are frustrated with us; we are too, which of course only adds to the pile of emotion we feel buried under. Sometimes we are grateful to feel empty and disconnected simply because the weight of our longing for the world, for energy, for something like happiness or just contentment is too exhausting to consider. We know already that we should be able to just "leave it at the foot of the cross" and "find our joy in Jesus." I promise you, we tried it, and the well is still dry.

Yet despite its frequent Pollyanna-like prescriptions, Christian practice and our holy Scripture have rich gifts to face the experience of depression. The roots of our faith are deep and can bear the weight, if only we will rest long enough in our faith's shade to recognize what gifts there are to receive. Perhaps we could take the psalmist as definitive *for* the experience of depression: If joy does not come with the morning, it is time for more action than simply a single night's rest.

The church—from ordained leadership to influencers of Christian culture, and everywhere between and around—should regularly gift those of us living with extended sadness or "depressed mood" with the truth of Scripture: Our grief, emptiness, impatience, and despair are common experiences by faithful people throughout the generations. Depression cannot be interpreted, from any biblical mindset, as a sign that God is absent or that the sufferer has somehow failed. We see the long-set grief of Naomi, husband and adult sons all buried in a foreign country, straggling home to Bethlehem with a gentile daughter-in-law in tow. The women of Bethlehem think they recognize her, but she is so changed by sadness that they are unsure: "Is this Naomi?" "Do not call me Pleasant," she responds. "Call be Bitter, for the Almighty has dealt bitterly with me."[5] Yet Naomi-now-Mara's anger with God is no grounds for her continued suffering; instead, she will find in her foreign daughter-in-law a way not only into a line of succession but into the very line that will produce the king David[6]. Naomi-now-Mara does not put her bitterness aside when she returns to her people; she is continuing to grieve, even more than ten years after her husband has died. Her bitterness is not condemned, nor does it cause a spiritual rift; it exists as a fact of the story, a judgment not against the grieving widow and childless mother but against God.

We might recognize too the depression caused by continued trauma, and the failure of substitute joys, in the story that immediately follows Naomi's—that of Hannah. Hannah has been childless for several years (a Jewish midrash says nineteen), and her husband has taken a second wife, who not only produces many children but also taunts Hannah for her own failure to conceive.[7] Years of childlessness—perhaps marked by miscarriages—and daily torment by her husband's other wife drive Hannah to weeping each year when her husband offers the sacrifice at Shiloh. He fails to understand her grief: "Hannah, am I not more to you than ten sons?"[8] In Hannah, we can recognize the compounding pain of repeat trauma, under which she does not become more resilient (as others might, and as some might expect or ask), but rather feels the sting more deeply each time. We also recognize in Hannah the failure of those closest to her to understand her weeping; her husband assumes that a double portion of the sacrificial meat, and his love for her, can surely make up for the house filled with children that are not hers.

One year, it all becomes too much for Hannah, who goes alone to the temple to weep and pray. Even there, she finds little comfort; the priest, Eli, assumes that her tears and soundless words are only evidence that she is drunk. Rather than take his shaming, she pushes back, stating without reserve that it is not wine that has brought her there, but a soul that needed "to be poured out before the Lord." A better priest than many who have followed in leadership, Eli immediately retracts his condemnation of her behavior and instead blesses her: "Go in peace; may the God of Israel grant what you have asked." Seen and recognized by the holiest man in Israel as a woman whose grief is real, Hannah is able to return home and to eat.[9] It is not the granting of her prayer that brings her peace, but rather that someone she knew to be faithful recognized that her pain was deserving of attention. We who live with depression can be deeply blessed by those who follow Eli's example and accompany us, even for a moment, in our silent, heart-wrenched prayers for alleviation of our pain.

We find the gifts of sadness, grief, despair, and depression embodied in many of the laments of the psalmists and prophets, who in faith and trust clung to the unfulfilled promises of God. Over and over, from individual betrayal to communal devastation, we hear the writers of Scripture name the internal wasteland of finding our hopes lost. *My eyes waste away with weeping; how long must I bear such pain in my soul? Tormented with loneliness, my friends stay far away; like a worthless shard of pottery, shame covers my face.*[10] There is no lack of grief in Scripture, and we should be ready and willing to put the words of God's people to our own experience as a remembrance that even in our loneliness we do not walk an unknown path. Faithful people of God have long tread with sadness and despair, and God walked with them. Jesus himself, to capture the complete abandonment and isolation of the cross, quotes from the psalms: *My God, my God, why have you forsaken me?*[11]

The majority of the lament psalms turn to praise, clinging to hope in God: *Hope in God, for I shall again praise the Lord, my help, my God.*[12] But one among them does not. The eighty-eighth psalm has no author attribution, no particular context for war or sickness, no fear of enemies or proclamation of righteousness. The unknown psalmist weaves their way through troubled sleep, weeping, guilt, isolation, exhaustion, and desperation. It is raw grief, desolation, and despair—and it has no resolution. No resolve of trust concludes it, no hope caps it; it remains open-ended. We cannot demand the psalmist cheer up, or call back through the ages "it could be worse!" It is holy Scripture, raw in its pain and challenging in its persistence.

Faithful Christians wanting to walk with those of us who know the journey of depression will need to practice the exhaustive patience of our own holy text. Do we have the faithful capacity to leave the psalmist where they are? Can we accept that not every sadness has a quick end, that not every weeping night sees joy rise at dawn? I invite you to wonder, at this moment, what can be said in the face of despair. What speaks good news for those of us who feel unyielding grief, or a strange numbness, or an exhaustion we cannot explain? Those called to walk with us can embody hope in a number of ways. Each chapter in this book ends with a series of questions;

those of us walking with mental illness might find it helpful to read them aloud to ourselves, and those invited to walk with us might practice and reach for them when the time is right.

QUESTIONS TO ASK

- What are you struggling to do, and can I help? *(Many of us living with depression feel overwhelmed by even the smallest mental or physical tasks—including scheduling an appointment with a doctor or therapist.)*
- Have you eaten today?
- Do you want to talk about it? *(Sometimes we can feel that our emotions are too much to share, either for ourselves to speak or for another person to hear. If we have the option to say "Yes" or "No" to sharing, it can give us a better grasp on what would actually help us.)*
- What helped the last time you felt like this? *(We can sometimes feel like we've never felt this bad or never gotten better, but depression can have significant variations in mood, and remembering that we have previously gotten out of this kind of "low" can give us hope.)*
- Is there a place you feel like you can be honest about how you're feeling? *(If the answer is "no," it might be time to activate a support network and help your loved one find a safe and honest place.)*
- Can I pray with you? *(This one is tricky—we who walk with mental illness can be skittish around invitations to prayer, because they've often come with the assumption that if the prayer doesn't "work," something is wrong with our faith. But prayer can also be a way of opening*

the door for true expression and a sense of being seen. Invite us to prayer only if you feel you can remain open and unresolved with us—we might not immediately experience a sense of release or peace, and it's important that we walk away feeling that's okay.)

FURTHER READING

On daily devotions on practicing self-appreciation: Henri Nouwen, *You Are the Beloved: Daily Meditations for Spiritual Living*, Convergent Books, 2017.

On gracious accompaniment in the midst of depression: Jessica Kantrowitz, *The Long Night: Readings and Stories to Help You through Depression*, Fortress Press, 2020.

On low times as a gift: Barbara Brown Taylor, *Learning to Walk in the Dark*, HarperOne, 2015.

On grief as a public gift of transformation: Soong-Chan Rah, *Prophetic Lament: A Call for Justice in Troubled Times*, InterVarsity Press, 2015.

CHAPTER FIVE

WORRY

"Does the Bible actually say 'Fear not' 365 times?"

Natalia is my pastoral colleague in more ways than one. We serve different congregations—mine, a one-pastor church in a community center in a city neighborhood; hers, a two-pastor multi-staff suburban church with a generous parking lot—but we share a sarcastic wit, a love for interactive worship, and a nasty streak of Enneagram 1 perfectionism that leads to a lot of "can you fact-check this quick?" texts.[1] We also share an immediate suspicion of anything that sounds theologically "tidy" when it comes to the Bible. It's a lot messier of a book than most of Christian culture likes to admit.

"Could be," I texted back, "but let me Google."

Any time a claim about the whole Bible sounds Pinterest-worthy, I think something's gone wrong in translation or interpretation. I wasn't surprised to find that the 365—or, as some influencers tried to say, 366, "to even cover leap years!"—

wasn't true. No one seems to be sure where the 365/366 claim came from. Varieties in interpretation and translation put the full count at somewhere over a hundred; it then appears that we have to add all instances of "fear God" or "I will trust in the Lord," from which we are supposed to infer that we should "fear not."

"But it doesn't matter!" wrote some apparently important Christian Instagrammer. "Even If God said just it ~once~, that's all that counts." I held back my thumbs from commenting, *The Bible also says only once not to wear gold, so what's with the jewelry multilevel marketing you're promoting?*[2] I knew being snarky wouldn't help. I get it. We want the Bible to be all things to all people: a science textbook, a truthful history, a magic eight ball that gives us the exact answer we need the first time we ask. We want our Scripture to be the perfect prescription against anxiety, so that God can tell us each day not to be afraid, like a page-a-day calendar for the desk of our minds. I would very much like that holy text, if anyone's got it. Instead, we have this jumbled-up record of sixty-six books with just as many (or more) authors, all trying to describe their experiences of faith with the one God they came to call Adonai, Jesus, Spirit. And in the midst of all that experience? Lots of fear, tons of worry, none of it a sign of their lack of faith. Perhaps the hundred-some utterances of "do not be afraid" might not be meant to shame those who live with anxiety and phobias.

Anxiety is a normal and common human emotion when we are faced with a change or a challenge. Moving to a new city, the first day of a new job, a high-stakes exam, preparing for a difficult conversation: All of these kick off an "anxious" response, which raises our awareness, expands our perception, and helps us adapt. That anxious feeling is supposed to help us focus, react, and improve. Where it goes haywire is when anxiety becomes an interference with everyday life; it might not come and go with specific higher-stress situations, but rather persist even when we're at rest and safe. Disordered anxiety can be so intense as to be debilitating, preventing a person from work, relationships, or even leaving our home.

Anxiety disorders take a multitude of forms. Anxiety might lead to panic attacks, where we experience a sudden onset of overwhelming anxiety and fear. In a panic attack, we might feel out of control or under the threat of impending doom; our hearts pound or race, we pour sweat or get chills, our breathing doesn't feel like it's working, our hands get numb, our chest hurts, or we feel sick to our stomach. In a panic attack, it's theorized, something has gone wrong in the brain to the point of serious terror, but the brain can't isolate *where* the threat is, so it activates a multitude of physical symptoms. *Is it here? Is it here? Look, I'm dying, it's got to be SOMEwhere!* Panic attacks can be entirely unpredictable, or can have seemingly random triggers (I get mine in grocery store checkouts, with no real personal experience to suggest I should be afraid of them), or can have a direct link to past experiences of trauma. Panic attacks can be so debilitating and terrifying that the fear of the next panic attack *causes a panic attack.*

Anxiety can also take the form of a *phobia*, a specific and irrational fear. A phobia manifests as intense fear and anxiety about a particular situation, object, or activity. Even thinking about the object of fear can kick off the fear and anxiety. Once again, this kind of fear is a dialed-up helpful emotion; fear of something that can hurt us is what historically and even today can save our life. Snakes? Might be venomous. Rustling tall grass? Could be a saber-toothed tiger. Speeding car? Move out of the way. Here, fear is not only natural, but necessary for life. But people with phobias will deliberately avoid contact with the thing that causes the irrational fear—like refusing to even look at a picture of a spider. They might know—or even be able to say out loud—that the spider cannot hurt them, but the phobic dial in the brain sends such an overwhelming set of symptoms that they cannot react rationally. Activating a phobia can be similar to activating a panic attack; physical symptoms erupt all over the body. Someone with a phobia might feel shaky, dizzy, or faint; they might feel like they are choking or can't breathe, go numb, pour sweat or get chills, feel sick to their stomach, or have a pounding heart or chest pain.

We see anxiety manifest in all sorts of often-parodied disorders, like obsessive-compulsion or hypochondria. In obsessive-compulsive disorder, or OCD, irrational fears are linked to specific and repeated behaviors, sometimes directly connected to the fear and sometimes only connected distantly. After I've checked the garage door once, my non-OCD brain goes: *done*. But someone living with OCD will not be able to turn off the cycle of *the garage door is open and a murderer will be hiding in my house when I return*. They may have to open and close the door a certain number of times, or touch the door when it is closed, or install security cameras that allow them to check again and again. In the same way, illness anxiety disorder (formerly known as hypochondria) is an irrational fear about symptoms, real or not, that point to chronic or fatal disease.

Another specific embodiment of anxiety can be found in social anxiety. An anxious feeling when meeting someone new, preparing for a first date, going to a job interview, or navigating a tough conversation with a friend or family member are all normal and common experiences of anxiety. We are social creatures, and a number of our social interactions have unspoken rules and high stakes. Social anxiety disorder distinguishes itself by encompassing these and also "everyday" activities—eating or drinking in front of other people, using a public restroom, making a phone call, going to school—in a collective cycle of fearing judgment, humiliation, and rejection. This anxiety does not go away after handling a particular situation but persists, getting in the way of going to work or school or facing any task that involves human interaction. We might worry ahead of time for weeks before something happens, or be seized with anxiety afterward about what we did or did not do and how others will react. We might avoid places, events, and people entirely. (At my worst points with my social anxiety when living alone, I would eat absolutely any concoction I could create from my fridge and pantry to avoid going to the store. Flour, olive oil, and water was a favorite to mix and fry to avoid having to buy anything that would constitute an actual meal.) The irrational fear is not the only symptom; as with other anxiety disorders, we with social anxiety can flush or get chills, have a pounding heart, feel our mind "going empty," get nauseated, and maintain a rigid body posture.

But don't worry (ha!)—if you're reading this list and feel that you experience anxiety without a particular situation like socializing or a jump-scare, there's also generalized anxiety, which can focus on almost any and all issues in life: money, health, family, work, politics, ecology. Once again, each of these issues is deserving of some degree of attention and adaptivity;

with generalized anxiety, the cycle of fear is so pervasive that the mind cannot move on, and the body can experience sweating, nightmares, a racing heart, shortness of breath, and fatigue.

Anxiety and phobias can be attributed to particular experiences—like a fear of dogs after one bit us as a child—or they can have seemingly no connection to our past. Two people can experience the same event—a dog bite, for example!—and one may walk away with related anxiety, and another may not.

Here is the secret we might not know how to tell you: We usually know our fears are irrational. I know that I am not going to die in the grocery checkout just because a stranger notices that I am packing my bags deliberately, and yet there is something like a fire alarm going off in my head while my hands start pouring sweat (which, in case you were wondering, does not help pack bags faster). I frequently tell myself, *We're okay. There are other checkouts. Other people are going at the same pace. Look, that guy's even slower! We are okay!* and yet while one part of me is detachedly soothing, another part is screaming and running in circles in my mind. Many of us who live with one form of anxiety or another are aware that our fear reactions and mental cycles are not responding to reality as it is. That experience can be even more distressing—to be caught in an anxiety spiral, to know that is what it is, and to *still* not be able to think our way out of it.

Because Scripture does not give us an extended internal view of its writers and actors, it is difficult to retroactively diagnose anyone in it with anxiety. Depression, or at least the symptoms of a depressed mood and extended sadness, can be found in expressions throughout the Bible, but perpetual fear of something that might not be an active danger is less commonly expressed. We might find instances of "anxiety" or "worry," like Martha fixated on her many ministry tasks or Jesus greatly troubled by the sisters' mourning of Lazarus,[3] but these are events with direct connections to reality. We do not have a biblical account of someone who experiences perpetual fear despite being physically safe and relieved of high-stress work. (Retroactive diagnosis of any mental illness is a tricky subject; we neither want to erase the existence of mental illness in history nor assume that our contemporary understandings have a full grasp of a long-lost person's internal emotional, mental, and spiritual life.)

We do, however, have biblical experiences of people who fear and worry. When we limit the Bible only to a proclamation of "fear not!" we ignore both the legitimate fears of the faithful *and* the proper place of God's invitations to step away from fear. In the book of Esther—a book in which, it should be noted, God never speaks nor acts—the newly crowned queen is in deep distress when her cousin and adoptive father Mordecai tells her of his rival Haman's evil plan to kill every Jewish person in Persia. When he begs her to go to the king and save her own people, Esther rebuffs him: "Anyone who goes to the inner court without being called is put to death, unless the king holds out his scepter and lets them live." Mordecai is consumed with terror at the coming destruction of his people; Esther is both horrified at what he tells her and fearful that any attempt she makes to change the king's mind will only result in her own demise as well. Mordecai—the story's exemplar of Jewish faith, who would not bow down to Haman even though it would have spared such anger—does not tell Esther, "Don't be afraid." He admits, openly, that she is in danger. What he invites her to instead is not ignorance of her own fear, but courage in the face of it: "Perhaps you have been made queen for just such a time as this."[4]

The multitude of *be not afraids* throughout Scripture echo and resound in Mordecai's pronouncement. "Be not afraid" is not a suppression of fear or a rejection of reality. Fear is a real response to a situation, and to the best of our knowledge, biblical fear is a rational reaction to a terrifying situation. "Do not be frightened or dismayed," says God to Joshua as the Israelites prepare for battle against much stronger enemies. "Do not fear," says the prophet Isaiah to the people in exile who have heard chapter after chapter of their communal sin and separation from God. "I will fear no evil," says the psalmist walking in the valley of death. "Why are you so afraid?" Jesus asks the disciples, quivering in the center of a boat nearly swamped by the sea. "Do not let your hearts be troubled," says Jesus to the disciples who have just heard he is about to die. "Be not afraid," says the radically transformed Son of Man, with skin like glowing bronze and hair white like wool.[5] It is not that the situation does not inspire real fear; it is rather that the imminent danger is not the end of the story. This is almost an entire reversal of the experience of anxiety, where the threat is not real and the fear cannot be overcome. Those of us who walk with chronic anxiety know too well that the assurance of "be not afraid," biblical or not, is not the magic key that unlocks our mental cycles and our pounding hearts. Instead, what is necessary can feel counterintuitive: to treat our anxiety as real even if the threat is not.

To treat our anxiety as real even if the threat is not, we step away from easy answers that might shame or exacerbate the cycle of panic and fear. We refuse to "diagnose" our anxiety as a symptom of spiritual failure or a need for more prayer or Bible study. In treating our anxiety as real, we recognize that we are experiencing both emotional and physical symptoms that are, in many ways, out of our control. Rather than denying or hiding the experience, we admit to what we are feeling. If you have been invited into this acknowledgment of our anxiety, we likely trust you a great deal or are in great distress (or, quite often, both). To walk alongside us in this journey, we will ask you, too, to treat our anxiety as real while recognizing that the threat is not.

The category of "anxiety disorders" is a long-term issue. Anxiety in the shape of mental illness is not a single experience of nerves before a big event or after a difficult experience. Anxiety has the possibility of chronic and recurring debilitation of our ability to participate in and enjoy all the aspects of human life, including navigable degrees of fear. Recognizing that anxiety does not disappear but requires sustained attention and care for recovery is necessary. Expectations, either from the person burdened by anxiety or those walking with us, of a "quick fix" from prayer *or* medication *or* the first session of therapy can only complicate and compound our experiences of self-doubt and shame, since we will be frustrated (and terrified) by the likely failure to recover immediately.

Detangling anxiety is a process. Before we can fully unweave the threads of irrational fear and worry, we will have to develop care practices for disrupting the cycles of anxiety. We may have to remove ourselves from anxiety-provoking situations at first, to prove to our mind and body that we have the ability to escape the "threat." Over time, we may be able (especially with work with a licensed and trained therapist, but also through other resources) to interrupt the cycles of panic and to practice enough mindfulness to calm down the body as we approach an event or object that triggers an anxiety response. Medications (once we navigate the process of finding a helpful doctor or psychiatrist and establish the right brand and dosage—a process requiring great patience in itself) can help lessen the immediate reaction of anxiety, which allows us to more directly deal with the irrational mental cycles rather than being trapped in them.

Compassion and patience will be, as with most mental illness experiences, the watchwords for those who accompany us on this journey. If something in spiritual thought or Christian practice falls into the category of triggering anxiety (for example, a repeat emphasis on our uncleanliness and unworthiness, which can prompt cycles of repetitive OCD behavior), church leaders and members may be challenged into rethinking how we frame and discuss our relationship with God as individuals and as a community. Perhaps, to those of us living with anxiety, the church can speak new good news: *Be not afraid of being afraid. Be not afraid of being honest with how your mind spins, for we can remain grounded while you find your roots again. Be not ashamed of worrying in a world that is sometimes truly scary. Be not afraid of being seen in the pharmacy drive-thru, for we will celebrate with you each day that the side effects have faded and the hope has remained. Be not afraid of being afraid, for it is no sign that God is gone but rather a door opening toward where God is leading.*

Be not afraid.

QUESTIONS TO ASK

- You seem [describe the behavior: tense, disconnected, upset]. Is something going on? Would you like to go somewhere else?
- What's making you feel unsafe?
- What's the message playing in your head?
- Do you want to talk through what's on your mind? *(Sometimes naming our anxieties out loud, and recognizing that they are real but the threat is not, can help slow the cycle of worry.)*
- Do you want to go for a walk? *(Getting away from a particular situation and spending time and energy in another direction can help stop the immediate cycle of worry.)*

"Grounding techniques" are simple practices for disrupting anxiety cycles and refocusing on the present. One well-known grounding technique is *"5-4-3-2-1."*
Name out loud:
5 things you can see
4 things you can feel
3 things you can hear
2 things you can smell
1 thing you can taste.

FURTHER READING

On integrating anxiety and theology: Jürgen Moltmann, *Experiences of God,* Fortress Press, 1988.

On practicing mindfulness: Ellie Roscher and Heidi Barr, *12 Tiny Things: Simple Ways to Live a More Intentional Life*, Broadleaf Books, 2021.

On anxiety in kids: Carrie Lewis, *All About Anxiety*, Beaming Books, 2020.

On anxiety and the church: Ryan Casey Waller, *Depression, Anxiety, and Other Things We Don't Want to Talk About*, Thomas Nelson, 2021.

CHAPTER SIX

PSYCHOSIS

"Can I ask a question?"

My proctor looked up.

I paused, feeling ridiculous. "Am I . . . how am I supposed to answer some of these questions?"

She gave me the kind of assessment that every tester fears: a detached gaze, waiting for me to dig the hole deeper.

"Like this one." I half-held out the booklet. "It says, 'I believe outside forces are controlling my life.'" I looked at her. "I mean—that's why I'm here. But I feel like I'm supposed to say *False*."

She looked back to her computer screen. "Yeah, that's not really what it's asking. Just . . . leave that part out of it."

That part, as far as I could tell, was that I was presently taking this exam because I wanted to become a pastor. *That part* meant God.

The MMPI (Minnesota Multiphasic Personality Inventory) is a psychological test meant to assess personality traits and the possibility of mental illness in a given individual. It was first designed to test those who were already suspected of having mental health issues, but has expanded in its scope to become a screening tool in careers—including, at least in 2010, for potential pastors in the Evangelical Lutheran Church in America. Obviously, the intent is to screen for mental illness and either treat or redirect a candidate for ministry, but I'd run into an issue: The line between being called by the Abrahamic God to serve the Christian church was, technically, indistinguishable from believing that cows were controlling my mind through the milk cartons in the grocery store.

I put down *False* and had a minor crisis of faith that day.[1]

When we hear the word *psychotic*, we think of a slew of violent and erratic behaviors: screaming and raging, breaking things, physical threats, stalking and monitoring another person. In the field of mental health, *psychosis* actually refers to a particular set of *internal* thoughts or personal experiences, rather than a set of externally observable behaviors. Of course, psychotic thoughts and internal experiences can be the catalyst for erratic or dangerous behaviors, but it is the individual's thoughts, not their actions, that are considered in the label of *psychosis*. In general, psychosis or psychotic episodes[2] have three sets of symptoms: hallucinations, delusions, and disorganized thoughts.

In *hallucinations*, a person experiences something that is not physically or "really" there. This is often auditory or visual, but it can involve any of our senses. Someone experiencing a hallucination might "hear" ordinary sounds, like doors closing or footsteps walking, or they might "hear" voices, including commands to take certain actions. Hallucinations can also take the form of lights or visual patterns, or physical beings from fungi to humans and everywhere in between. A hallucination might feel like floating or being outside your own body, or a crawling feeling on your skin. Hallucinations can be caused by existing mental illness, but also by fatigue, dehydration, substance abuse, detox, or migraines. A person experiencing hallucinations may be able to understand that what they are seeing, hearing, or sensing is not based in reality, or they may not be able to distinguish between the two.

In *delusions*, a person holds a false belief that persists in spite of evidence. The belief is patently false, and yet the person believing it is convicted of its truth. This is not because of a person's level of intelligence or education, or because of culture or religion; it is false because of some anomaly in their process of thinking. They will continue to believe in the delusion despite repeated evidence shown to the contrary. These delusions can take a host of forms. A person experiencing delusions might feel paranoid or trapped, believing that someone (or everyone!) is out to get them or is intentionally mistreating them. These are sometimes called *persecutory delusions*. Someone with persecutory delusions might believe they are being followed or spied on, or tricked or ridiculed, or that their partner is cheating on them. Another common form of delusions are *referential*, seeing patterns in books or newspapers, gestures or comments, or other cues from the environment that have a secret code or contain instructions for the person experiencing the delusion. *Grandiose delusions* are beliefs that the person has special powers or talents or abilities, or is in a relationship with someone famous, or has a specific, wide-reaching, and powerful role to play in the world. Some delusions might defy reality on multiple levels, like mind control or telekinesis. Not all delusions fall into neat categories; they only require that the person experiencing them is absolutely convinced of their reality despite all evidence to the contrary and any negative effects that believing them has on their life.

The third set of symptoms in psychosis has a variety of names, but most commonly is typed as *disorganized thoughts*. People with psychosis can have patterns of thought that are somehow disturbed or disrupted. Sometimes it feels like thoughts are going through one's head so fast that they are out of control, or that the thoughts bounce from idea to idea so quickly that meaning is inferred where others do not see it. A person experiencing disorganized thoughts may speak very quickly and stumble over their words, to the point that other people cannot follow along. They may jump from topic to topic suddenly in conversation, following how quickly their thoughts are moving, and may find it difficult to keep attention on one thing. Some people experiencing disorganized thinking may create sentences based on how words sound rather than what they mean, which makes their speech sound jumbled to others. Disorganized thought may also mean that someone suddenly loses their train of thought and cannot return to it, but also cannot switch to another thought, which causes an abrupt and disruptive stop in conversation or activity.

The collection of experiences that make up psychosis can have a number of potential causes. Like many symptoms of mental illness, genetics appears to play some factor. Traumatic events—the death of a loved one, the experience of war, a sexual assault—can be the root cause for the disconnect with reality experienced in psychosis. Psychosis can also arise from major physical illness or injury: traumatic brain injuries, brain tumors, strokes, brain diseases such as Parkinson's or various forms of dementia, and HIV. Substance use can cause not only psychotic experiences while intoxicated or when "sobering up," but can also change the brain chemistry to the extent that psychotic experiences continue even into sobriety.

These are all independent experiences of psychosis, but sometimes it is a symptom of a larger mental health concern, such as schizophrenia, schizoaffective disorder, bipolar disorder, or depression. Hallucinations, for example, are experienced most commonly in schizophrenia. At present, psychologists understand schizophrenia to exist along a diverse spectrum. Within that category of mental illnesses, schizophrenia itself is serious and long term, in which delusions, hallucinations, and disorganized thought cause consistent and long-term impairments in the ability to function socially and physically. Schizoaffective disorder shares many symptoms with schizophrenia, but also has symptoms of mood disorders—usually of bipolar (episodes of mania and depression) and of "depressive type" (only major depressive episodes). Also within the cluster of schizophrenia is schizotypal personality disorder, in which there are brief experiences of psychosis (but not as prolonged or intense as schizophrenia) along with impaired social abilities.

The delusions, hallucinations, and disorganized thinking of psychosis (whether experienced as part of a mental illness, or as another physical illness or event) can also produce "negative symptoms"—instances in which a particular aspect of ordinary human life is removed. Many people with psychosis withdraw socially, not understanding how relationships form, how to trust another person, or how to interpret another person's motivations correctly. They may appear to "lack emotion," or have emotional responses to social cues that others find confusing or inappropriate (like smiling when told about the death of a loved one). Some people with psychosis, particularly if showing other symptoms of schizophrenia, may refuse to make eye contact or will speak in a monotone voice. Others, sometimes those diagnosed with schizotypal personality disorder, have a deep social anxiety and avoid social situations.

Experiences of psychosis, and the spectrum of mental illnesses of which they are a symptom, are deeply troubling both to those who have them and to their loved ones. Some people are able to distinguish between their psychosis and reality, while others not only cannot but are deeply shaken (even enraged) by contradictions. Prolonged psychosis can disrupt every aspect of life, from family and interpersonal relationships to the capacity to maintain employment and safe housing. Yet culturally, we hear "psychotic" used as a descriptor of an ex-girlfriend who would really like her ex to pay back the money she lent before he ghosted and blocked her. We jokingly post the gif of Charlie Kelly in *It's Always Sunny in Philadelphia* standing in front of a wall full of articles, maps, and photos, with dramatic red yarn connecting all of them—neglecting to remember that some people, including friends and family and fellow Christians, live with a mind that sees illogical connections and believes in them so strongly that it isolates the person from their loved ones. Even the words "psychotic episode" spark in us not compassion for the tragedy of un-reality, but an image of someone whose words and actions are unpredictable, out of control, and dangerous.

And yet, in the context of religious belief, the experiences of psychosis take on a completely different meaning. Moses had heard the stories of the God of his Hebrew ancestors, but that belief was newly embodied when he saw a bush ablaze without being consumed. Moses returned to Egypt and proclaimed to his people that he had met the Lord, whose name was Being, and who had chosen this adopted grandchild of Pharaoh, this exiled murderer turned desert shepherd, to lead the people out of bondage.[3] Moses's vision and importance are distinct from hallucination and delusion because others experienced them with him—his brother Aaron also heard and witnessed the Lord; the leaders of Israel saw the signs Moses was given; the whole of Egypt was plagued by the result of Pharaoh's repeated refusal to let the people go.[4] Even in receiving the gift of Torah, the five books of the Law which begin the Hebrew Bible (what Christians call the Old Testament), Moses did not witness God alone; sometimes he was accompanied by Aaron, sometimes by Joshua, sometimes by the elders of Israel.

But Moses reignited a long train of Hebrew ancestors who had experienced a direct intervention by the divine into their ordinary reality, in which not everyone would participate. His reinvigoration of the Abrahamic faith would lay the work for other prophets to come. At a young age, the boy Samuel, dedicated to the service of God by his mother Hannah, directly heard the call of the Lord that his master Eli did not.[5] Samuel then became the prominent prophet and judge of Israel, negotiating between God and the people as they recommitted to serving the Lord alone and, at the end of Samuel's life, ask for a king to rule over them. In these negotiations, Samuel took no one with him, but reported back all that God had said.[6] God then chose the young man Saul as the first king of Israel, possessing him with a "prophetic frenzy" as confirmation of Samuel's anointing.[7] But Saul, who never himself heard the word of God, eventually went against Samuel's instructions; the spirit of God then left him, and instead "an evil spirit from the Lord" tormented him. (A shepherd boy named David—the newly and secretly anointed king of Israel—was able to ease the evil spirit with music.)[8] The prophetic work passed from Samuel into relative quiet until the rise of the prophet Nathan, who spoke for God in regards to David's plans for the temple ("no") and David's rape of Bathsheba and slaughter of her husband Uriah ("absolutely no").[9]

Samuel and Nathan received the word of God independent of the perception of others, and served as judge for a people and a guide for kings. In their footsteps followed many of the other prophets of the people of Israel—Elijah hearing the voice of God in the great silence on Horeb, Isaiah who sees the six-winged seraphs around the throne, Ezekiel who tasted the scroll and found it sweet like honey.[10] These prophets had intense and reality-defying experiences of the divine, which confirmed their place as prophets and guides to the chosen people of God. Their prophecies were rich with metaphor, alternately comforting and chilling; they were often ostracized from family and found themselves on the fringes of social and religious practice because their proclamations disturbed both loved ones and people in power. Scripture holds hundreds of faithful reports of phantasmal experiences, from the terrifying visions of Revelation to the gentle voice of Gabriel singing, "Hail, Mary."

We know this from our own faithful experiences, too. Many of us have known the strange familiarity of the sudden and inexplicable presence of a loved one who has died. Others among us have been struck with an awareness of powerful evil around us, or found ourselves in a full-body sensory experience of grace and love. Otherworldly, unreal, miraculous: We try to find words to explain how it is that we sensed, or saw, or heard something that we knew was not there and yet could not deny the physical and mental effects it had on us. Yet we also know that others who experience "un-reality" can do so in ways that are harmful to themselves and others—and even insist that their experiences of psychosis are faithful manifestations of the divine. How do we safely and compassionately distinguish the holy visions of the prophets, the fleeting experiences of our own longing hearts, and what medical and psychological assessments might characterize as "psychosis"?

First: **Does the person insist their experience is "real"?** Someone grieving the recent death of a parent might say, "I know she wasn't there, but I could smell Mom's perfume." But many experiences of psychosis, because they pair hallucination and delusion, mean that the person experiencing them cannot distinguish between what *seems* real and what *is* real. When someone insists that their experience is real, despite all evidence to the contrary—such as demanding to know who is hiding upstairs because they could hear footsteps, or explaining that they are the secretary to the treasury for the president—we might distinguish that as an experience of psychosis. A key part of treatment in addressing psychosis is reaching a stage at which hallucinations and delusions may still happen but can be understood as distinct from and not bearing on reality.

Second: **Does the experience cause psychological distress?** Many of the aspects of psychosis are disturbing and disruptive for the person experiencing them. Some experience paranoia and heightened anxiety, fearful that everyone is out to get them; others might experience a state of mania, in which they feel powerful and untouchable; still others might feel unable to move, stymied by racing and seemingly unconnected thoughts. The psychological distress of psychosis may be apparent to the person experiencing it, or they may feel that their disconnection from reality has granted them special privilege or skills. If the disconnect from reality either causes emotional or mental distress, *or* has an impact (such as bodily harm or manic behaviors that lead to financial debt or destroyed relationships) that causes distress as a result, we may be seeing an experience of psychosis rather than a religious vision. Of course, religious visions can be challenging both to self or to community; prophets rarely bear a proclamation of divine approval! The prophetic experience is often rich in metaphor revealing something about our existing reality, but then asks for concrete action in real-world terms. The paranoia and mania that frequently characterize experiences of psychosis may be helpful in making this distinction. Biblical prophets spoke in metaphor, but also found ways to state their fears of the future with concrete examples and acknowledged that not all people would be able to understand or accept what they said. A person experiencing psychosis may not think of themselves as "distressed," but they might be obsessively distrustful or unable to accept the existence of criticism. If someone speaking as a "prophet" insists that nonexistent forces are trying to silence them, or rejects any detractors as obvious and universal heretics, we may be observing psychological distress.

Third: **Does the experience ask the person to commit harm to themselves or others?** While the biblical prophets often *predicted* harm to come for an individual or community because of their break in the covenant or their oppression of the poor, the prophet was not chosen as the *agent* of that harm. Jeremiah's rotten loincloth and oxen yoke, while uncomfortable, did not cause immediate or lasting damage to his body.[11] Experiences that ask the person having them to do violence to themselves or others are far more likely to fall into the category of psychosis than religious vision. One complication in this question is that some who experience psychosis do not believe that violence on their part would actually constitute harm of another person. A caregiver who believes they must physically harm a child in order to protect them from nonexistent evil forces does not think they are hurting the child; they think they are helping. Assessment of "harm" takes a whole community, not just one individual. Metaphorically, if a hundred people can see a house and only one sees a fire, we do not allow that one person to axe in the door and turn a hose on the furniture.

Finally: **Is the "unreal" experience helpful for the community?** Prophetic visions and the divine anointing of leaders have a purpose: to deliver a whole community. Moses did not receive the name of God to make him special, but to be able to communicate with the Divine who sought to bring their people out of slavery and teach them a new and liberated way of life. Experiences of un-reality that only seek to privilege a particular person, or to give them insight that does not benefit anyone but the individual, are less likely to be religious visions. This is, once again, difficult to distinguish since the person experiencing un-reality may very seriously believe they are receiving a revelation. (Tragically, we see this all too often in leaders of cults, who sincerely believe their version of reality is helpful to others and convince others to share in the delusion and trust the hallucinations; the cult then creates a structure in which those un-realities cannot be questioned.) A fellow Bible study attendee at my high school once told me I couldn't *actually* have depression, because she could see demons and I didn't have any. Surely she felt she was helping me, but what was actually happening was a denial of my own reality (serious symptoms of depression) as subject to her experience of un-reality. Without the discernment of a whole community, empowered to confirm or reject an unreal experience, the centering of one particular person's experience can become dangerous fast. Perhaps Paul got it right for once: "let two or three prophets speak, and let the others weigh what is said."[12]

Note that these are not meant as diagnostic questions; they are suggestions for determining, within a community where religious visions can happen, whether an experience of un-reality is Spirit-led or psychosis-related. In many cases, someone experiencing psychosis will not be able to distinguish between the two. What, then, do we do as individuals and as faith communities to support the person experiencing psychosis without normalizing their unreal experience or allowing them to harm themselves or others because of it?

Support the use of medications. Many people who experience psychosis find relief in treatment with antipsychotic medications. These used to have drastic side effects (so those who have taken them in decades past may have horror stories to tell) but are continuing to improve in efficacy with fewer side effects. Antidepressants or mood stabilizers can also help the mood disorders associated with psychosis. Many people experiencing psychosis may believe they are better off without medication, or that they can "handle it," which highlights the importance of faithful support for the use of medication as a mitigator for psychosis.

Champion counseling. Supportive counseling with a licensed therapist trained in handling psychosis is crucial to developing the emotional and mental strength a person experiencing psychosis will need. Occupational therapists and social workers can also help someone experiencing psychosis to handle life skills such as finding a job, managing their finances, and connecting with community services. Normalize therapy as something that everyone can benefit from, not a treatment reserved only for serious problems.

Intervene early. Knowing early signs of psychosis, and taking steps to connect someone experiencing them with a trusted doctor, can reduce the chances of intense or prolonged psychosis. Most practitioners suggest we help someone connect with a trusted doctor or therapist if they begin to share mistrustful or paranoid beliefs, have unexpected emotional outbursts, begin to isolate from friends and family, or have noticeable changes in their mood or habits (from sudden elation, to emotional flatness, to no longer performing basic hygiene needs).

Approach with care and non-judgment. People experiencing psychosis are often distrustful and will not reach out for help; they may be confused and distraught by their experiences and try to keep them secret. If you want to approach someone about their experiences and your concerns, prepare to do so in a space that is private, free of distractions, and not closed in (to reduce any feeling of being "trapped"). Try to mirror their behavior; if they avoid eye contact, do not force it; do not touch them without invitation and consent. Name the specific beliefs and behaviors that worry you; you don't need to speculate about a diagnosis, or question their medication regimen.

Practice patience. People experiencing psychosis are often unable to think or speak clearly. When disorganized thinking disrupts their ability to communicate clearly, speak in a straightforward and succinct manner, and be prepared to repeat things if necessary. Allow them plenty of time to process what you are saying, even if they are showing a limited range of emotion.

Do not focus on the experiences of psychosis. Delusions and hallucinations feel very real to the person experiencing them. Dismissing or arguing about them will only augment their distress and disconnect, as will acting horrified or alarmed by the experiences. At the same time, treating the experiences as if they are real—if I had asked my dad to point out where the chicken was, and then looked in that direction—can undermine recovery as it creates a link between reality and un-reality that becomes difficult to sever. Although we may be very curious as to what the person is experiencing, or want to "prove" that they are wrong, either of these can be seriously destabilizing. If someone describes an experience of psychosis, try to remain as neutral as possible, and steer the conversation back toward shared reality.

Know who to call in an emergency. People across the spectrum of mental illness can fear interactions with police, and psychosis can elevate and intensify that fear. If someone is threatening to harm themselves or others (due to psychosis or, really, for any reason), know who in your community is safe to call: which emergency services prioritize medical care over policing, or what organizations have social workers and trained de-escalators available. If you are meeting with someone who experiences psychosis, make sure that both of you can step out of the situation if it becomes unsafe (not meeting in a room with only one door, for example).

Remember that you cannot do everything. There is only one savior in the world—and although you are wonderful and capable, it is not you. Saving and redemptive care for someone experiencing psychosis will not involve only one person, but a whole community of support structures.

QUESTIONS TO ASK

- What will help you feel safe and in control?
- Is there someone I can call that has helped before—a family member, a friend, your doctor? *(Give concrete examples of who might be able to help.)*
- How would you like to be helped?
- What has helped you when you felt like this before?

FURTHER READING

Simonetta Carr, *Broken Pieces and the God Who Mends Them: Schizophrenia through a Mother's Eyes*, P & R Publishing, 2019.

Adam Lambsin, *Schizophrenia, Mental Illness, and Pastoral Care*, WestBowPress, 2016.

E. Fuller Torrey, *Surviving Schizophrenia, 7th Edition: A Family Manual*, Harper Collins, 2019.

CHAPTER SEVEN

TRAUMA

Around Valentine's Day, two out of three years, "turn the other cheek" comes knocking rudely on the church door, demanding to be read. The lectionary calendar—the planned set of readings for each Sunday and feast day that hundreds of thousands of Christian communities around the world use—sets Matthew 5:38–42 and Luke 6:27–31 in the season of Epiphany, the time between Christmas and Lent when we focus on Jesus's early healings and teachings. In the hardest part of my Minnesota winters, when the bitter cold compels me to give up on cross-country skiing or any other ludicrous snow sport that we've made up to convince ourselves we actually like the icy weather, when I could really use a flicker of hope, the church instead sets my teeth on edge with "turn the other cheek."

So it seems only fair that, two out of three years, sometime around Valentine's Day, I invite a member of the church to take a swing at me.

The Christian church has too long used this idea of "turn the other cheek" to insist that the abused must submit to the abuser, that the victim must return to their suffering, that there is no protection for those who come to faith seeking deliverance. So it seems right to let someone take a swing at the pastor.

Usually the volunteer is whichever child feels most spunky that day. This year, it was Auggie. Auggie was not yet of an age to understand how to fake a punch, so I had to drop myself backward and out of the way when he threw his right hook. He and the congregation all erupted into laughter. Then I slowly walked him through what it would be like to hit me on the other side of my face—what he would have to do if he was going to hit me with his right hand on my *right* cheek: "If someone strikes you on your right cheek, turn the other also." A punch would not land nearly as solidly from a right hand to a right cheek. "If you wanted to put some power behind it, you'd have to backhand me." (More giggles.) And he sure did. This time, when I threw myself backward, I felt the *whiff* of his fingers across the front of my nose, and I could hear the congregation gasp while they laughed, realizing how close I'd come to being clocked by a six-year-old.

And then I say, every two out of three years: This is what it looks like to turn the other cheek. A right hand to a right cheek would be a backhand. Historically, we understand this gesture to be one between two people unequal in power—a master to a slave, a husband to a wife, an adult to a child. But to turn the *other* cheek, to force the attacker to hit with their right hand on the *left*, would be a punch or an open-handed slap—a gesture between equals. Turning the other cheek, perhaps, was not about meekly submitting to the violence of another person, but rather, in refusing to fight back, still stating: *I will not allow you to treat me as someone lesser than you. I will remind you that we are both equal before God.*[1]

The base definition of trauma is an emotional and physical response to an extremely negative event. Most of us go through trauma, at some point; we face serious illness, we mourn the death of a loved one, we witness a serious accident or violent attack. Our emotions afterward can be unpredictable and seemingly irrational, but they are actually a reflection of the event. A sudden flat affect or emotional "emptiness" protects us from the extreme emotions we might fear feeling; displaced anger can be a sign of our disruption and sense of lost control; jumpiness or heightened reactivity shows the effect of a sudden spike in our stress hormones. Our ability to recognize and respond to traumatic events, and to try to predict or avoid them in the future, is one of the things that helps us survive—both in history as humanity evolved, and in our present-day societal and individual lives. A not insignificant amount of behavior can be traced to our pressing desire to not be hurt.

When trauma takes a step into mental illness is when the normal reactions—a fender-bender that encourages a little more caution when merging—are severe and prolonged enough to interfere in everyday life—such as being too afraid to get behind the wheel at all. There is no precise calculus for which traumatic events will cause lasting trauma in a particular person. Even genetically related family members will handle traumatic stress in markedly different ways, even to the point that one person may experience lasting trauma and one may not.

Lasting trauma can arise from a number of situations. Common causes of trauma are immediate threats to physical safety—intimate partner violence, sexual assault and rape, surviving a natural disaster, facing a serious illness. Trauma can result from one single event (sometimes called *acute trauma*), or from repeat events (sometimes called *chronic trauma*), such as long-term abuse or serving in armed combat. Trauma does not have to cause actual physical harm to a person for trauma symptoms to arise: the sudden death of a loved one, for example, or repeat verbal and emotional abuse. Witnessing an act of violence against someone else can also give way to trauma symptoms (sometimes called *secondary trauma* or *vicarious trauma*). We see secondary trauma symptoms in the emotional and physical effects on Black communities when another instance of white supremacist police brutality is widely publicized. Children are particularly susceptible to trauma, for a number of reasons: They are deeply dependent on caregivers, which augments the effects of abuse or neglect; their brains and bodies are still developing; their smaller size and experience makes them easier targets for violent and prolonged abuse. Children who have experienced trauma are statistically much more likely to be re-traumatized in youth and adulthood.

Emotional, mental, and psychological responses to trauma run an extensive spectrum. A traumatized person might experience denial and numbness, sadness and depression, anxiety and fear, guilt or shame (especially if they survived an event that others did not, or if they feel they somehow caused the event), anger and irritability, confusion, hopelessness, and difficulty concentrating. There may be emotional outbursts or a sense of being overwhelmed by conflicting emotions; they may withdraw from other people. Flashbacks and nightmares where the traumatic event is relived are common. As with much of mental illness, there are physical responses too. Trauma can cause exhaustion and fatigue, or inexplicable headaches; there might also be digestive symptoms. Someone might experience hyperarousal, where their body is on constant alert: a racing heart, sweating, jumpiness, inability to sleep.

Diagnosis of a trauma-related mental illness is complex and varied. In post-traumatic stress disorder, or PTSD, a specific traumatic event creates a brain "loop" in which the immediate stress caused by the event is repeated over and over throughout the next weeks, months, and years. Once again, the experience or witnessing of trauma and the immediate reactions—what we sometimes call "fight or flight," or "fight, flight, freeze, or fawn"—are normal, common, and self-protective. It is the chronic and debilitating repetition of those reactions, in cases where physical danger is no longer apparent, where fear has gone from "normal" to "disordered." PTSD is commonly characterized by intrusive memories (like flashbacks, unwanted recall, and dreams and nightmares); avoidance (refusing to think or talk about the event and avoiding places, people, or activities similar to it); negative thought and mood (including hopelessness, self-depreciation, memory problems, relationship difficulties, detachment, and emotional numbness), and "arousal symptoms" (easily startled or frightened, often on edge, trouble sleeping or concentrating, irritability or outbursts of anger, and self-destructive behavior). Complex PTSD arises from multiple traumatic events—like abuse, intimate partner or community violence, or war—and shares many symptoms with PTSD (sometimes called, to distinguish it, *uncomplicated PTSD*), including impulsivity, intense emotion, substance abuse, depression, and panic. The many symptoms of prolonged trauma directly contribute to the rise of other mental illnesses, ranging from depression and anxiety to borderline or antisocial personality disorder to substance abuse.

Like many other mental illnesses, prolonged trauma puts pressure not only on the sufferer but on their care system. Because others did not react in the same way to a similar situation, or because they were not present at all for the trauma, family, friends, and fellow church members can be confused and frustrated by trauma responses. They may not realize someone has trauma, and therefore be caught off guard by a seemingly sudden explosion of emotion from someone feeling trapped by a re-traumatizing situation. The impulsivity, self-deprecation, and detachment that often characterize trauma can splinter relationships. Meanwhile, the traumatized person's own frustration with their inability to "move on" grows. "Let go and let God," says the poster on the church library wall, where someone has their back pressed into the old wood paneling so hard you can trace the knots of wood imprinted on the back of their arms because they don't feel safe unless they can see every corner of a room. Once again, the church will offer what has been helpful for others, but find its resources coming up short when the simple answers no longer hold.

Christian culture can provide a variety of responses to trauma—not all of them helpful. Simultaneous with its confession that "all have sinned and fallen short of the glory of God," much of the church seeks to recognize the goodness in each person—either inherent to their existence or as a result of their salvation and sanctification—and celebrate it. This is not a failing in the church as a whole, but it can cause us to misinterpret situations of abuse. Unable to recognize that a person could be capable of inflicting trauma on another person, we simply refuse to accept that abuse or neglect has happened.

We might even find ourselves giving into an ecclesiological form of *gaslighting*, a term which has entered public vocabulary in recent decades. In the 1944 film *Gaslight*, Ingrid Bergman's character is subject to a manipulative and violent husband who turns down their gas-powered lights (along with making noises in odd parts of the house); when she asks him to confirm the dimming lights and strange sounds, he denies them and claims she is going insane. "Gaslighting" as a term has thus come to represent when a person or people deliberately and secretly cause self-doubt and confusion in another person or people, making the victim(s) question their own memory or perception. Gaslighting augments trauma; when we deny the reality of another person, we increase their own emotional, mental, and physiological trauma by telling them that what hurt them *did not actually happen.* "He didn't mean it that way," we might say, or "she couldn't have done that." Unfortunately, this can take on even more nefarious forms when it is blended with faith: "but she's a good Christian," "but he goes to Bible study weekly," "but they're a leader in the church."

Gaslighting can take another and seriously more toxic form within Christian practice, which has sometimes been called "God-willing." Instead of denying that the event happened, as one would do in gaslighting, in this case a person reinterprets a traumatic event to say that *it was God's will.* This then delegitimizes the trauma of the event, since it is no longer traumatic but rather a "gift from God." One might point to, for example, the suffering of Job as a test of his faith for which he is rewarded; another might cite the story of Joseph: "what you intended for harm, God intended for good."[2] Anyone still suffering from the trauma of the event is thus shamed into ignoring their mental and physical symptoms since they do not reflect Paul's assertion that "suffering produces character." If the traumatic event was God's will, then we should have no traumatic symptoms!

What gaslighting and God-willing both do is to shift the problem of blame from the abuser to the victim. Both frameworks for denying trauma recognize that people fall short of the glory of God, but they assign the guilt of sin on the person who is in pain, not the person who caused the pain. This can happen for a variety of reasons. We may have given too far into the belief that every human being is good, and therefore be unable to recognize when someone else has fallen short. We may have bought too firmly into an optimistic vision of the church as a peaceable kingdom, in which case we are afraid to bring up conflict or deal with confrontation. We might ourselves have been victimized and traumatized in the past, but it is too hard for us to deal with the effects of those events, so we have to deny the trauma of people in the present as well. We may be frustrated by the impulsive or self-destructive behaviors of a person with trauma and therefore ascribe respect and authority to the person who is behaving "rationally"—the abuser. We may also feel helpless in the face of someone else's revealed trauma. We may be dealing with a situation in which it seems impossible to restore justice for the victim—whether this is because the trauma happened so far in the past that reparations seem unattainable, or the person who caused the trauma is in such a position of power and authority that to approach them directly about their behavior seems unimaginable.

What systems in secular society and in the church often do is problematize the victim. Because we cannot manage the symptoms of trauma nor figure out a way to restore justice to survivors, we make the hurt people the problem. We see this for example in the historical biblical treatment of eunuchs—men who had been castrated. Castration was performed by someone else, often (unsurprisingly) against the man's will. Eunuchs were valuable in political and royal areas of life; they could be close to the king and queen without being a danger to "contaminating the royal line." Because they could sire no family of their own, they were considered more loyal to the royal family. Castration was common in many ancient societies including Egypt, Babylonia, the Persian Empire, and Rome—all conquerors and oppressors, at one time or another, of the Hebrew people. Thus, we find in Hebrew law a prohibition against eunuchs as members of the religious community: "no one whose testicles are crushed or whose penis is cut off shall be admitted to the assembly of the Lord."[3] These were men who had been conscripted into service of foreign powers and foreign gods; their servitude had contaminated them, and would endanger the whole community if they were included. But note that they had not volunteered for castration—they had been violated, and then were violated again by their own people in their exclusion. The judgment that had been issued against eunuchs was not a reflection of their own sinfulness, but a re-victimization of those who had gone through severe trauma. Perhaps this was part of the reason for God's fierce proclamation through the prophet Isaiah:

> Do not let the eunuch say 'I am just a dry tree.' For thus says the Lord: to the eunuchs who keep my sabbaths, who choose the things that please me and hold fast my covenant, I will give, in my house and within my walls, a monument and a name better than sons and daughters. I will give them an everlasting name that shall not be cut off.[4]

Is it so far outside the realm of possibility that God would take the side of the victim?

We can also see the effects of problematizing the victim in systems, especially within churches, that focus on forgiveness as the primary source of restoration in systems of abuse. Too often the Christian prescription for abuse has been to "forgive like Jesus, seventy times seven," without acknowledging the verses that come immediately prior: where the victim comes to the violator, sometimes with community support, and tells them what has been done, and the violator listens and repents.[5] When our systems of restoration focus only on forgiveness, we risk re-traumatizing the victim and perpetuating the systems of abuse. Faced with women who had been objectified as sexual objects or "caught in adultery" but brought to him suspiciously alone, Jesus refused to participate in re-victimization. *Take out your own eye if it's such a problem. Whoever is without sin can be the first to cast the stone.*[6] The work of forgiveness, according to Jesus, is to unbind what has been bound—yet our fear of confrontation and our culturally adopted practices of problematizing the victim can do the exact opposite of what forgiveness aims to, and keep people bound in their trauma.

But how can we condemn trauma when its very violence is central to our faith? At the front of almost every Christian church is the embodied confession that trauma can be for our good—in the horizontal and vertical stripes of the cross. Jesus himself said, "take up your cross and follow me," indicating that his followers would suffer to be true disciples. Trauma might not be a gift from God, but couldn't it be simply a fact of following Jesus—one that we cannot expect to lessen in our lifetime, one that we should bear with joy since it makes us like Christ? This was long a dominant strain in Christian theology, especially as we conscripted young men into the colonization and genocide of "other people" in far-off lands. Suffering and death were nothing compared with the glory won in Christ by our march into trauma and the destruction of cultures and people before us. We interpreted the cross, very early, as a sign of redemptive suffering, and believed it to be active in us too.

James Cone famously reframed the violence of the cross as a redemptive *public* act. Jesus's death was not salvific because he balanced out the "sin account" of all of humanity, but rather because in the state-sanctioned and public nature of Jesus's death, we saw, as did America in the murder of Emmett Till (and Trayvon Martin, and Sandra Bland, and George Floyd), the wretchedness of our own sin laid bare.[7] The creator of the universe had walked among us with a message of mercy and abundant grace, and we—religious authorities, political powers, ordinary people turned screaming crowd—killed him. Faced with our own unredeemable sins, we were finally compelled to do something different.

But in a prescription of redemptive suffering as the lens to interpret trauma, we fail to notice when trauma is private. Forcing an abused woman to return to her husband because it is "her duty to God" does nothing salvific. It allows the husband to persist in his sin, it dooms the children to their own cycles of trauma, and it denies the image of God in the woman who has just been told her own pain is nothing compared to the potential of her husband's reform. Womanist— Black feminist—theologians, in particular, pushed back on Cone's theology.

That same womanist work aligned, in some ways, with the liberation theologies arising in South America, where the local leaders of Catholic churches had begun rejecting long-taught atonement theories that glorified suffering and promised the least of these that they were "like Christ." A rapid decline in economic self-sufficiency, a militant increase in political repression and violence, and the torture and assassination of political opponents were categorized by the ruling classes as "a cross to bear" for the majority-Catholic poor. Instead, these priests, nuns, and laypeople came to recognize that the suffering Christ underwent was not a justification of all pain but rather a divine solidarity with the oppressed and marginalized. When God put on skin, it was to join in with all those who had been crushed, and reveal the sinfulness of those in power and their systems of abuse. Suffering is not redemptive in and of itself; it *can* be redemptive when it transforms those who witness it, but this cannot be faithfully done if it endangers the life of a beloved child of God. To believe that those suffering under the burden of abuse, neglect, and re-traumatization must return to their own pain and allow it to fester, without promise of restoration or deliverance, is to deny the truth of God's protective love. It would be better to have a rock tied around our necks.

What would it look like instead to practice a Christianity that was tender around trauma? Recently, the expression *trauma-informed* has become part of therapeutic practice. Trauma-informed care recognizes the widespread existence of trauma, works to recognize and identify symptoms of trauma in people and systems, and implements practices to avoid re-traumatization. To help individuals in navigating their past trauma and to reduce future abuse and neglect in our congregations and spiritual practice would be a fuller expression of God's love and of the protective care we are called to show for each other.

Our cultural, Christian, and individual hesitancy to talk about trauma does not make it less real. The CDC reports that at least one in seven children has experienced trauma or neglect in the past year, and estimates that number may be actually higher.[8] About one in four women and nearly one in ten men will experience physical, sexual, or psychological violence by an intimate partner.[9] Nearly one in five women have experienced attempted or completed rape; of those, one in three was assaulted before they were eighteen, and one in eight was assaulted before age ten. Men report sexual assault at significantly lower levels, though statisticians suspect this is because of cultural shame around male rape. Of the men who do report having experienced sexual violence, one in four was assaulted before age ten.[10] Trauma is widespread. Refusing to attend to it within Christian circles because "it doesn't happen here" is a straightforward denial of reality.

When we make ourselves open to the existence of trauma, we are likely to hear stories that deeply shake us. Those of us who are trusted with the honor of hearing a survivor's story may feel an immediate surge of protective anger and hunger for justice, or we may be shocked and not know how to respond. Our call is to stay present with the survivor in their experience, not to center our own. When the conversation is over, we can seek a trusted partner to share our own shock, horror, or grief at what has happened, but when someone is baring a deep wound, our challenge is to keep our own emotions at bay as best we can, and provide a safe and nonreactive space for them to process and unburden themselves.

For those sharing prolonged effects of trauma, we can help navigate a self-care plan for addressing its symptoms. For those sharing ongoing trauma, we may want to immediately jump to a solution—"You have to leave him now!"—but this can be counterproductive, because we mirror the experience of trauma by removing their sense of control and direction for their own life. We can help in developing a safety plan for escaping abuse, with the tragic knowledge that many people who have experienced trauma will return to it again. Breaking off a relationship requires financial and emotional independence that many people experiencing abuse may not have access to; in addition, when a survivor decides to leave an abusive relationship is statistically a high point for intimate partner violence.[11] Whether we are walking with someone who has borne past abuse or who is experiencing trauma in the present, we will need to rely on a great deal of patience. Healing the scars of trauma is a long-term process, which will require systems of self-care that go beyond one person.

A crucial step in treating trauma as real and reducing its prevalence in the future is for every church and Christian group to actively prevent assault and abuse within its community. Volunteers and leadership should be expected to submit to background checks. Policies that explicitly name sexual, physical, and emotional assault, especially in regards to children and youth, with clear paths for reporting—and with concrete and transparent follow-through—can empower victims to report behavior that crosses boundaries, offering victims and those who care for them the opportunity to intervene before trauma becomes prolonged. Prevention and treatment of abuse will also involve full community education about the warning signs of intimate partner violence, abuse of children, and grooming behaviors of predators. Many denominations offer "safe church" or "boundary" trainings that help leaders and volunteers identify unhealthy patterns of behavior and set up guidelines for reducing opportunities for trauma. This can include basic standards for care of children and youth, such as not having a single youth and a single adult alone in any situations, but also can teach how to appropriately respond to allegations of abuse in ways that protect the victim and prevent re-traumatization. But all of this will require serious self- and community reflection on our theology around bodies, restoration, and justice, and the church has often feared and avoided this work.

The Christian church has feared and avoided reflection on much of its body theology because it has significantly benefited from rejecting individual body autonomy. To some extent, the early church required such a rejection; its survival and its ability to care for its members relied on wealthy and powerful members giving up their own wants in order to provide for the needs of the whole. But over time, this generous and Spirit-led impulse became an expectation and a demand, handed down from the powerful to the powerless. The marginalized—women, people of color, the disabled community—have been expected to submit to the ruling classes of the faithful, who established and reinforced systems in which women were second-class, people of color were naturally "lesser," and the disabled community was disempowered and hidden away. Many systems of evangelism and ministry rely on individuals giving up their own autonomy—working for no pay "for the gospel," for example, even though leaders at higher levels draw a full salary.

The concept of body autonomy is also outright rejected in some circles of Christianity for its connection with the pro-choice movement. "You do not have authority over your own body," says this theology; "it belongs to your husband and/or to God." Attempting autonomy over your own body—even just to say you do not want certain types of sexual contact, or that you cannot work fifty hours in a week—can be reframed as rejecting God's rule, which is intimately connected with the rule of whatever humans are in power in that particular church or faith community. But body autonomy, the right to say "No" when we do not want to be used or hurt, is core to who we are as beings created in God's image and reflects the long arc of God's liberating work.

To assume that human authority or individual power to overcome another person's own autonomy is indicative of the will of God ignores the trajectory of the story of the Exodus, in which God directly intervenes to fight back against structures of abuse and trauma. God, through Moses, declares to the Hebrew children: *You are right. Egypt's rule is horrific, and it will now come to an end.* Their suffering is not a gift from God meant to test their faith, nor is it a result of their sinfulness and their own self-victimization. God rejects their suffering as redemptive or meaningful. Their trauma is simply *wrong*, and it is time for the source of abuse and pain to be drowned in the depths of the sea. When we refuse to speak up in the face of abuse, when we giggle awkwardly at any mention of sex in sermons, when our children do not feel that they can say "No" to hugs from a stranger at the passing of the peace, are we participating in Egypt's silencing of the Hebrew children?

Trauma-informed Christianity will also require our own awareness of how we have focused on forgiveness of the perpetrator rather than healing, protection, and restoration for the victim. At the shores of the Red Sea, God does not tell Moses, "Go back and try one more time. Forgive Pharaoh. Maybe this time he will be compassionate." God has witnessed what too many of us know to be true: The cycle of abuse is more likely to continue than to stop. Trauma cannot be prevented by subjugating ourselves to suffering over and over again. At some point, we cannot continue trying to negotiate with power that will not listen. At some point, it is time to leave and not look back.

We will also be called, in the face of trauma, to practice true justice and accountability. There will be nothing to all our work around trauma prevention if, when abuse in the church is reported, we silence the victim and shelter the abuser in committees and "sabbaticals." If we do not follow through on policies meant to protect against trauma, we will be complicit in re-traumatizing the victim. True justice will only come when we are willing to face how our own participation in and reliance on systems of power can make us want to avoid confrontation. The lessons of the wilderness wanderings after the exodus, the complaints and the rebukes, the stories and laws, were intended to protect a community that only knew power and abuse. *No, you will not live like Egypt*, said God through Moses and the other leaders. *You will learn a different way, where you will not hoard bread or land, where you leave grain behind for the poor to gather.* Certainly the provisions that they made do not perfectly transcribe to four thousand years later; it would be abusive today to require a victim to marry her rapist.[12] But for the time, it is possible that the provisions of Deuteronomy meant that a man would not be permitted to abuse a woman and then abandon her to lifelong shame. In the same way, we will be asked to reconsider our policies, our practices, and our teachings around authority, autonomy, and abuse, so that we do not perpetuate the victimization of the past but continue to protect the least of these among us.

Auggie, by his own decision, doesn't receive communion yet. He comes forward with his hands firmly at his sides, ready for his blessing.

"Is it okay if I put my hand on your head?" I ask him. We do this every Sunday. For Auggie, it is as sacred a part of the ritual as the blessing itself. He laughingly corrected a visiting pastor who foolishly reached for his forehead before asking. Today, he gives me a grin and nods. I lower my hand to his head and trace a cross with my thumb: "You are a beloved child of God, and Jesus loves you very much." He grins again, and scampers along.

I turn to his brother Joey, who by *his* own decision, does receive. I think about what it means to tell a ten-year-old that the creator of the universe had to be broken into bits because of how awful we all are. How if we do not eat his body, we have no share with him. How we drink his blood.

"The body of Christ," I tell him, holding up a torn piece of bread between our meeting eyes, "a promise of God's love for you."

QUESTIONS TO ASK

People who have experienced trauma may have "triggers"— sensations or situations that set off trauma responses and emotional outbursts. If you think someone is experiencing one, you can try: You seem like you're [describe behavior—becoming distant, feeling frustrated, getting anxious]. Do you want to take a quick walk with me and reset?

For someone currently living in an abusive situation:

- I don't have all the answers, but do you want to make a plan together for how you can get safe when you're ready?
- What do *you* want your life and future to look like?
- What do you think God's hope for your life is?
- Is there an image of God that helps you feel safe?

FURTHER READING

On understanding the complex symptoms of trauma: Bessel van der Kolk, *The Body Keeps the Score: Brain, Mind, and Body in the Healing of Trauma*, Penguin Books, 2015.

On re-traumatization through church theology, and how it might be transformed: Rita Nakashima Brock and Rebecca Ann Parker, *Proverbs of Ashes: Violence, Redemptive Suffering, and the Search for What Saves Us*, Beacon Press, 2002.

On abuse within the church: Emily Joy Allison, *#ChurchToo: How Purity Culture Upholds Abuse and How to Find Healing*, Broadleaf Books, 2021.

CHAPTER EIGHT
FOOD

The first thing I ever gave up for Lent was candy. I don't remember the year, but considering I grew up with a religious streak a go-the-extra mile wide, it was probably before I turned ten. At some point, I learned that Lent was about giving something up, something special but something you could certainly live without. I don't remember how I chose candy; someone must have suggested it—maybe my mother, maybe one of the priests at our Episcopal church. It's a pretty simple idea, giving up candy, and certainly not a bad one for a kid with a sweet tooth. So I gave up candy one year, sugar the next. At school my circle of friends, most of them some mix of Protestant or Catholic, would recite what they'd given up too. We'd mention it casually over the middle school lunch table, in between sharing Chapsticks and gossip. We didn't complain—after all, Jesus didn't eat *anything* for *forty* days; it wasn't that much of a sacrifice to give up a trip to the vending machine for Starbursts.

Eighth grade was the year Lent lost its luster. Lent is anti-luster, right down to the way we start it: with ashes on our foreheads, the proclamation *Remember you are dust* ringing in our ears. Eighth grade was the year I accidentally brushed my face after morning service, leaving most of the ashes stuck to my fingers and a faint streak across my nose. My mother wordlessly gave me a Kleenex to wipe the rest of it off my face before she dropped me off at school. I stared into the flip-down car mirror. This was holy stuff, this ash. I wasn't supposed to just . . . take it off. If I took it off before I went to school, didn't that mean I was ashamed of being a Christian? And how would I throw it away? Usually I washed it off at night; mixing ash with water and sending it down the drain was not nearly as unsanctified, I felt, as wiping it off with a Kleenex and tossing it in the school garbage. But I also couldn't leave a smudge across my face. It didn't even look like an ash mark anymore; it looked like I'd been trying to do a smokey eye and missed.

I wiped it off and tucked the Kleenex in my backpack. I'd heard about how to dispose of holy things appropriately: worn out Bibles, hole-filled American flags. I'd sneak it home and burn it later. My mother probably did not need to know about this. She also did not need to know I snuck a Jolly Rancher from the backseat stash. If I'd already ruined Lent by messing up my ashes, what was the point of giving up sugar?

This would be the best-case scenario for seeing through the holes of Lenten sacrifices: Sometimes it doesn't take, for whatever reason, and we remember that grace is abundant.

But the ashy Kleenex and the Jolly Rancher wrapper were just the start of self-discipline falling apart.

"I'm going to give up Channel 2," Kelsey laughed through her sandwich.

"The Sesame Street station?" we asked, staring at her.

"Yes." She finished her bite and swallowed. "My pastor said we had to give something up, so I'm giving up Channel 2."

"Do you *watch* Channel 2?"

"He didn't ask that," she said with a smirk.

I waited for a lightning bolt to strike her down. How dare she be so flippant about Lent? This was supposed to be about Jesus, not gaming the system. But I didn't have any jurisdiction to judge. I'd failed before I'd even gotten out of the church parking lot.

"I'm not going to eat from sunup to sundown," Christina told us, as easily as Kelsey had mentioned Channel 2.

I looked at her blankly. "That sounds like just not eating?" I mumbled.

"It's okay," she explained over the din of the cafeteria, "because I'll eat breakfast before dawn and dinner after sunset. Lots of people do it."

I didn't know how to say that I didn't believe her. We'd learned in health class that one of the ways girls with eating disorders hide their anorexia is to say at school that they ate at home, and say at home that they ate at school. I stared down at my lunch, my appetite lost.

"Yeah, my youth group did that," added Kelsey. "We didn't eat for 30 hours. We packed groceries for people. It was so hard. I was so hungry!"

"It's not that hard," Christina said. "You just have to put your mind to it. Jesus gave up everything for us. And I could stand to lose the weight."

And every girl at that table nodded, knowingly. At fourteen, ranging wildly in our conclusion of puberty, covering every size in the Forever 21 aisles, pushing each other on the fourth lap around the track to finish the mile in under eight minutes—as far as standing to lose some weight went, we thought we all could.

Clearly identifying the widespread crisis of disordered eating in America is a statistical nightmare. There are millions of patients, and most are invisible. In our diet-centric culture, disordered eating is not a sickness, but an expectation. We joke that we've been "bad" about our meals—as if produce hand-picked by human beings for well below minimum wage is somehow more ethical than a pricey pastry from a local bakery. How do you teach a society that disordered eating is a disease when every January 1 brings with it thousands of social media posts stacked with numbers: calories, miles, minutes on the mat. The clinical model of "disordered eating," where someone can be diagnosed by a medical professional, puts estimates in the "several millions" in America—ranging from eight million to twenty-eight million[1]. Statistically, most are teen girls and young women. But every girl at that cafeteria table nodded, having already bought into the belief that our bodies were in need of improvement.

Another reason disordered eating is difficult to track is its variety of symptoms. In some, we see restrictive eating and significant weight loss, most often diagnosed as anorexia nervosa (or "anorexia" in shorthand). The calculation of anorexia is simple: eat less, lose weight. Over time, without enough caloric intake to maintain our current size, our bodies will start to use "fat stores"—the evolutionary successes that allowed us to survive lean harvests and long winters. Weight fluctuation, and the existence of fat on our bodies, is not just natural, but was necessary for our survival. But the obsessive nature of anorexia destroys a person's capacity to recognize and understand their own body. Many anorexics suffer from body dysmorphic disorder—a fixation on the defects of the body, and specifically for anorexics, the belief that one's weight is excessive even when it isn't. Anorexics often deny that they are thin, even when their weight is significantly lower than is safe for their age, height, and other physical factors. (How do you diagnose *that* when few women would dare the social shame of agreeing that they look skinny?)

In the past twenty years, the dramatic rise in disordered eating, particularly the restrictions and food obsession of anorexia, prompted numerous education campaigns during my young adulthood, with publications of books like *Reviving Ophelia: Saving the Selves of Adolescent Girls.*[2] Anorexia is also considered to be one of the deadliest of mental illnesses; the caloric deprivation shrinks the brain, damages the skeletal system, and contributes to chronic infertility. When left untreated, anorexia can cause lasting or even fatal heart disease; the body, having consumed all its fat reserves, begins to eat its own muscles to survive.

Anorexia, for many, is how we envision disordered eating: a young woman, bones jutting out at uncomfortable angles, no energy or passion for participating in the world around her. Yet this image bears two contradictory lies: first, that such deprivation is an isolated choice rather than a consequence of a weight-focused culture; and second, that anorexia is common. In actuality, only *6 percent* of those diagnosed with disordered eating are clinically underweight.[3]

Disordered eating is far more varied than anorexia. Statistically—and perfect statistics, again, remain elusive—the number of people living with either bulimia nervosa or binge eating disorder is two to three times higher than those with anorexia.[4] Bulimia nervosa is characterized by cycles of binge eating and "compensatory behavior" to rid the body of food. Bulimia is most often imagined as purging through self-induced vomiting, but other practices include abusing laxatives or diuretics, fasting, or intense exercise. (How *does* one diagnose this when it's perfectly culturally appropriate to say, "I'm only having seconds because I'm going to the gym later!"). But even in seeking to educate and treat, our cultural images for disordered eating center those who are underweight, rather than the much more significant population of people living with an eating disorder while being average or above average weight.

At what is often stereotyped as the opposite end of disordered eating is binge eating. While anorexia and the purging cycles of bulimia are either whispered about or worried over, disordered eating that takes place in binges is often laughed at, because it is associated with obesity and the laziness and lack of control we blame for it. Consider Thor's weight gain in the Marvel movie *Avengers: Endgame*; it's a point of laughter, not a cause for concern.

Disordered eating, however, encompasses much more than just three separate categories. Many of those who live with disordered eating experience different phases of anorexia, bulimia, and/or binge eating, rather than only one of them. There are other types of disordered eating, such as avoidant or restrictive intake (sometimes in conjunction with autism) or orthorexia (seeking weight loss and restriction under the guise of "being healthy" or "clean eating"). Some kinds of disordered eating don't fit neatly into categories, or bear more resemblance to compulsive disorders than to disordered eating (like pica or trichophagia for example—eating things that aren't food). Relationships with food are complex—and in the midst of it all, there's Lent.

Lent is one of the oldest seasons of the Christian church calendar. Before there were New Year's Resolutions, there was Lent—a time of self-reflection, penance, charity, and yes, fasting. The church set aside the forty days before Easter (not counting Sundays) as a time for reflecting on and preparing for the passion of Jesus, the story of the betrayal, crucifixion, death, and resurrection of the savior of the world.

The forty days of Lent are meant to mirror Jesus's forty days in the wilderness. At the very beginning of his ministry, after being baptized by John, the heavens split open and God declared, "This is my son, the beloved; with him I am well pleased." Jesus then went into the desert, alone and isolated, and without food or water, to face temptation and discover what he would do with the power granted him as God's son.[5] In the gospels of Matthew and Luke, the devil's first temptation is for the starving Jesus to turn stones into bread. Where's the harm in that, after all? God made everything; why not use that power to rearrange some atoms? There are starving people all across the world; why not make bread enough to feed them? But Jesus quotes Deuteronomy: "One does not live by bread alone, but by every word that comes from the mouth of God."[6]

And so, two thousand years later, I gave up Jolly Ranchers and Christina gave up eating altogether.

Of course, it isn't fair to blame Lent for any of this. A practice of self-reflection and transformation, of self-restraint for the sake of another in need, of self-denial to focus less on a fleeting desire and more on discipleship—little of this is rotten in its theology. We, each one of us, need time to look into a spiritual mirror and take stock of what has taken the place of love of God and love of neighbor as ourselves. By setting aside a specific season of the calendar, the church confessed in practice what it knew to be true in philosophy: None of us are regularly at our best; other idols will perpetually seek to topple the liberating God and set themselves up in our hearts instead; we are called not into isolation but into community where the needs of the least are recognized and met and the power of the most privileged is used to change the brokenness of society. Preparing for Easter is not about dyeing eggs but about dying to our own sick hunger for power and control. Power and control in the hands of humanity is what tried to strike God down, only to find three days later that love does not stay dead. But this is difficult to teach a ten-year-old or a fourteen-year-old or, sometimes, a forty-year-old, and so Lent becomes a time to give up chocolate, and its end is celebrated by an extra-large basket from the Easter Bunny.

Lent isn't to blame for any of this. Our relationship with food is complex, because food is deeply tied to what it means to be human. Food is symbolic, laden with emotion, rich with memory. We eat because we are hungry, but we also eat (or do not eat) because we are scared, or anxious, or bored, or angry, or feel like there is nothing we can control. Disordered eating looks like a relationship with food, and the relationship with food will need treatment—but at its heart, disordered eating is about how we understand who we are and what we feel, and how to live with those feelings. *Am I worthy? Am I lovable, and loved? Do I have agency over my body and my life? Can I find ways to self-soothe when my emotions feel out of control?* The less we can answer "yes" to these questions, the more fraught our relationship with food can become. But asking those questions of ourselves, and listening to the answers, is a lot harder than giving in to the cultural offering of "if you're sad, buy a pint of ice cream."

Beyond our own relationship with food, we have an additional cultural layer to contend with. The seeming restraint of those classified as "thin" is given moral and ethical weight, as if every story of a thin person is that they can refrain from consuming what we mere mortals could never live without. In reality, there are certainly cases in which a person achieves or maintains a smaller body through avoiding certain foods or qualities, but just as frequent are the stories of people whose bodies are larger than they (and/or society) might prefer because of genetic predisposition or present hormone levels. Add to that the ability to exercise and eat a particular diet (whether keto, paleo, vegan, or detox)—an ability that culturally we expect everyone to have, ignoring the inherent costs. To exercise, one must have a place to do so and the energy and time to do it. Single parents working two jobs to provide for kids who also need a guardian at home and observant any

hour that they are not in school will have a hard time finding time, energy, and space for exercise. This does not dis-
count that some people do it! But just as many, or more, find
that there is little indoor exercise that their weary bodies can
participate in while also remaining quiet enough that barely
sleeping children are not stirred. Combine that with the existence of what we casually call "cheap calories"—carbohydrates,
sugars, and fats, which are lower in cost and provide more
instant energy than their nutrient-rich but expensive competi-
tors in fruits, vegetables, and meats—and we create a system
in which people already marginalized by poverty and circum-
stance are additionally culturally shamed for weight gain that
may be outside their control.

Fasting, throughout the world, is meant to focus our
attention away from ourselves and into the places of great
need and pain. Fasting is meant to provide a space for experienced solidarity with the poor, for clarity of thought around
what is a need and what is a want, for self-restraint when our
own greed—for money, for power, for whatever idol trying to
call our heart home—has tried to indulge. But what fasting
turned into, in American Christianity gone hand-in-hand with
American standards of beauty, is an unholy union of demonizing the body and prioritizing our own self-improvement over
the actual needs of the world. I do not believe Jesus cares what
number is on my scale, so long as I have my body employed in
care for creation and for God's beloved children. I want to take
Christina's face in my hands and say, "You are not Jesus in the
wilderness. You are not Elijah running from King Ahab.[7] You
are a middle-schooler in the American Midwest. Your body is
not even postpubescent. Your brain is more than ten years off

from full psychological development. And you are a beautiful and beloved child of God who simply by existing *deserves to eat some fucking lunch.*"

But to be able to speak that, the church will have to let go of a few things.

We will need to release our demonization of the flesh, and reach instead for holy relationship with the body. Christianity shames the body, right on back to Paul's hatred of the "flesh" and love of the "spirit," but that's not an easy separation within first-century Jewish thought (or within Jewish thought today). The necessary interrelationship between body and mind for the existence of a whole human being is inherent in the Hebrew Bible: There, we find no easy division between flesh and spirit, but rather a constant cycle of relationship between breath and animating force, between abstract words such as *nefesh* and *ruach* and *neshamah*, where existence and soulfulness is rooted in the aliveness of the body. Splitting spirit and flesh is not quite so easy as Paul, whose thorn should have taught him better, might have wanted to think. Our bodies are affected by our minds, and our minds are affected by our bodies.

The church would need to let go of an understanding of the body as evil and inclined toward sinfulness, and the mind as somehow "pure," and recognize instead that we are a whole being created as such—heart, soul, mind, and strength. All of it can be bent toward malice; all of it can also be fertile ground for goodness. All of it was made in the image of God. When we were created in the image of God, it was not an action to only create our minds but to create our whole bodies. The problem may not necessarily be with the flesh. The woman and man of the story of the Fall do not eat from the tree because their bodies are hungry (there is plenty of other food in the garden), but because their minds are fearful of death, and the snake promises the fruit as a way out. Is this not in so many ways the fear that drives us—that at the end of it all, we are fallible, we are weak, we will not live forever? If we are to embrace a holy approach to the body, we recognize that we will not forever be in a body (so our fears of that body's destruction cannot be the only rule of life), *and* we are now in a body (so we cannot treat the body as unnecessary).

We are now in bodies, bodies created by God—even inhabited by God. Jesus had hands and feet, ears and lips. Jesus, at one point or another, probably stubbed his toe or hammered his thumb. Jesus, at one point, might have had some extra skin around his tummy. Jesus was not by any scriptural accounts particularly outstanding in the looks department; after all, when the Roman soldiers come to arrest him, he just looks like any other Jew among those gathered at the Mount of Olives. It is only Judas's kiss that can identify him. What is it like to remember that God chose a body that was, by all accounts, undesirable—no Roman citizen privilege, no thin lips or pale skin, no Nordic characteristics we'd paint on him in later centuries? He was the standard of his day: Jewish, dark-haired, unremarkable in appearance. He is never identified by how handsomely he stands out in a crowd. What is it like to imagine that Jesus was plain? What might it be like to step away from not only an idealized standard for ourselves, but an idealized standard for our savior?

To practice a holy relationship with our God-made, God-worn bodies, the Christian faith and practice will also need to let go of its aversion to food. We might, for example, celebrate the many stories of feasts and parties throughout Scripture. We might meditate on God's provision of not only a flat, vaguely honey-flavored *manna*, but also rich-tasting quail across each square foot of the camp.[8] God is not a God of scraps. God is a God of abundant food, to the point at which we are more than satisfied. God sets out tables wide enough to feed all people with rich food and well-aged wine, with milk and wine free for the taking for anyone who comes hungry.[9] Can we actually believe in that lavish kind of God? Can we believe the prophet, that at this feast nothing tastes like junk food, but rather every calorie feeds us, sustains us, nourishes us, fills us? Can we act like God wants us to eat?

In Jesus's parables, when God's kingdom is depicted as a dinner, there are no scraps or small provisions. God does not withhold, it seems, either on grace or on good wine. God provides lavishly for the people who have come around the feast. It is not a scrap, it is a king's party, to which many are invited. Can we envision a God who fills the heavenly table, not just with flat-pressed discs of communion wafers and wine cheap enough to buy in bulk, but rather foods so lavish we can hardly speak of them, a feast that nourishes us in such a way that we are sent into the world fulfilled and full-filled?

And finally, if the church, Christian culture, and our individual practice are to shed our intentional or unintentional bondage with disordered eating, we will be called to embrace instead a holy fasting from injustice. Is this not, after all, what God calls us to? The prophets proclaimed over and over how disinterested God was in our bodily sacrifices, how disgusted the Holy One was when we thought ourselves righteous because we fasted while starving out the poor. Isaiah cast a vision of flowing waters and a feast of rich food, but despaired at the continued idolatry of child-consuming gods and the crushing suffering of those on the edges. *Why do we fast, but you do not see?* he quoted mockingly, only to cry out: *You fast just to serve your own interests and oppress all those who work for you! Will you call sackcloth and ashes a day acceptable to God? Is not this the fast that I choose: to loose the bonds of injustice, to undo the thongs of the yoke, to let the oppressed go free, and to break every yoke?*[10] Over and over throughout the prophetic writings in the Hebrew Bible, God turns away from feasts where food is distributed unequally. This was what fasting, in its best and righteous way, could actually do: bring us into solidarity and unity with those who did not have enough, and then to act on their behalf in the world, so that injustice would no longer reign and justice instead would pour down from heaven.

Of course, this is rarely how we approach fasting. But could we? What would it be like to consume the food that we do with attention to how and where it was produced—whether those who planted it, grew it, picked it, shipped it, delivered it, sold it were compensated fairly for their work? Are the animals cared for? Are the farming and harvesting restorative and sustainable, or is it simply consuming more and more in a way that we cannot maintain, and yet fool ourselves into thinking that we can by stocking our grocery stores and closing our minds to the suffering of the producers?

Could we fast from injustice and feast on liberation, not just for the food that we consume but also in every area of our lives—to dedicate ourselves in Lent, and in every season of the church year, to think through: What is it that we consume?

What is it that we think is feeding us? The doomscrolling on Facebook, the messages we play over and over in our own minds. What are we feeding our heart-mind-soul-strength? What are we starving others of?

We will never be able to bring the kingdom fully on earth—yet we will also not be exempt from the question: Where are we still feasting on injustice? Where are we still allowing ourselves to be filled (physically or metaphorically) by the suffering of others, especially when systems are set up so that we do not have to witness such suffering? This question will press on us, because the answers to it are uncomfortable. Those of us who benefit from being classed as white in this country will have to question in what ways that feast of privilege starves out those who are not white. Those of us who have disposable income, who have the opportunities that wealth can bring, will be pressed on how to support and create systems of mutual aid—in which we understand our wealth not as something to be distributed without attention, but rather to be sown as seeds into communities where they can grow up and fill, not just immediately but also sustainably.

When we ask ourselves what it looks like to fast from injustice and feast in the kingdom of God, we must simultaneously remember what it is to eat here on Earth. We have bodies; we are embodied. To eat—carbs and veggies and fats, fruits and sugars and proteins—is part of life. It was necessary even for God-in-skin to eat, to lounge on his side at a table with sinners and tax collectors, to make the best wine when everyone was already drunk. How we eat—how our food is sourced, and who has access to it— may be a moral question, but to eat itself is not a moral weight. While we work to better know what it is to fast from injustice, we will need to eat, to sustain and enliven our bodies for the work of knowing ourselves and caring for our neighbor, so that we continue to reach for a world where all may be fed.

QUESTIONS TO ASK

Realigning a disordered relationship to eating and food takes time. The following are questions that family, friends, pastors, therapists, and patients themselves might ask in order to help in the journey.

- Is there something that keeps bothering you? *(Disordered eating is about food, but it's often also a response to another situation.)*
- How do you talk to your body? How would you feel if a friend talked to their body that way?
- When do you feel most calm and comfortable?
- What would you feel comfortable eating right now? *(Forcing someone to eat, except when overseen by doctors and nutritionists, is extremely discouraged.)*
- When do you feel worthy of love and acceptance?
- What part(s) of the human body do you think is made in God's image? *(Developing a positive view of bodies in general can be part of recovery.)*
- How can I support you?

*It should be noted here that what we **don't** say can be less important than what we **do** say. Shaming ourselves for eating— "I'm gonna be bad and get fries!"—sends the message that we* *consider particular foods to have moral values. Openly talking about weight loss, reciting the calories of foods, or shaming yourself or others for the way their body looks and moves also contribute to disordered eating.*

FURTHER READING

On acceptance and Christianity: J. Nicole Morgan, *Fat and Faithful: Learning to Love Our Bodies, Our Neighbors, and Ourselves*, Fortress Press, 2018.

On the history of anti-body theology in Christianity: Michelle Mary Lelwica, *Shameful Bodies: Religion and the Culture of Physical Improvement*, Bloomsbury Academic, 2017.

On building body positivity: Sonya Renee Taylor, *The Body Is Not an Apology: The Power of Radical Self-Love*, Berrett-Koehler Publishers, 2018.

CHAPTER NINE

ADDICTION

I am making a second pot of coffee to finish the chapter on addiction.

Our images and understandings of addiction are complex and contradictory. Some addictive substances—stimulant or opioid medications, for example—are highly regulated. Some— like marijuana—are hotly debated, and punishment for their possession or use viciously demonstrates holes in our justice system. Cocaine drives entire systems of crime and economy; alcohol, tobacco, and gambling are legal as long as you're of age. Compulsive eating is a throwaway joke, while compulsive exercise is envied. And if I post a picture of my multiple empty mugs to Instagram, most of the responses will be laughter or commiseration. As a culture and a world, we put substances into our bodies and brains regularly without fully understanding what processes we might be contributing to—especially in the context of faith.

Addiction, or what is sometimes termed substance use disorder, is a complex series of beliefs and behaviors, primarily defined by the uncontrolled use of a substance despite its harmful present or future consequences. Addicts have an intense focus on using that substance, to the point at which their ability to function in day-to-day life is impaired. Even when they know that the substance is causing or will cause problems, they continue to seek out and use it, often in increasing amounts over long periods of time. They may downplay their desire for the substance or dismiss how their behavior causes problems.

Although addiction is usually defined in relationship to a "substance," the object of addiction can take many forms. People can develop addictions to plant- or fungi-based substances like tobacco or marijuana or "shrooms," or to concentrated chemicals like cocaine, PCP, LSD, and inhalants (like paint thinners or glue). Addictions can also be found in the misuse of prescribed medications, including opioid painkillers (especially codeine, oxycodone, and heroin), sedatives for treating anxiety, stimulants like ADHD medications (especially those that include amphetamine) or caffeine. A person can become addicted to food or to exercise, to gambling or to sex, even to their phone and social media. Whether these substances are "natural" or lab-made, whether they are chemicals we ingest or activities we partake in, has much less importance than what they do to our brains and bodies.

Addiction is a chronic disorder with a multitude of factors: our biology, our psychology, our social and environmental risk factors. Addiction is often experienced as a genetic trait, but also a behavioral one; a child might have genetic risk factors for addiction but also be exposed early on to substance abuse as a way of coping with stress. Any substance use alters our brain and body chemistry, at least momentarily, from the suppression of "still tired!" messaging through caffeine or the relaxation of alcohol. Addiction occurs when the brain and body respond more significantly to that alteration, craving that same "reward" chemical on repeat. That reward chemical can change our brain wiring around motivation, memory, impulse control, and judgment, with increases in cravings for the reward (in part due to growing tolerance from long-term use) and impaired ability to regulate use of the substance.

An addictive craving can be due to genetic predisposition, life experiences, or continued use (I didn't get a headache from not drinking coffee the day after my very first Starbucks, but you bet I'd get one tomorrow after sixteen years of two cups a morning). Stress, accessibility, and other environmental factors can make a mind and body crave another experience with a rewarding substance; there isn't a perfect calculus for why one person can drink two beers and stop, while another cannot stop until they black out.

Addiction does not develop in a vacuum. While there are cases of addiction developing from exposure to an addictive substance through curiosity or peer pressure, what is more common is for addiction to arise as a solution to emotional, mental, or physical stress. Addiction might develop when someone seeks a substance to relieve stress, block out problems, or feel numb; conversely, someone might seek repeat substance use to feel a pleasurable high that increases positive emotions, such as the rush of success when gambling or the heightened sensations of hallucinogens. In cases of stimulants, such as caffeine or amphetamines, a person might develop an addiction in the course of trying to improve their performance or thought process. Addiction to opioid painkillers can often begin in prescribed treatment after injury or surgery.

Essentially, a mind and body are better primed to develop an addiction when there is a recurring stress that they want to avoid, but do not have accessible solutions for. An accessible solution is, at baseline, one that someone can financially afford (especially with respect to health care access) and physically achieve (Is it handicap accessible? Can it be time managed around work and childcare?). Addicts seek a substance or an experience because what is accessible in their immediate environment and mental capacity does not give them the relief that they need. Unsurprisingly, then, addiction is often deeply connected with other categories of mental illness; psychiatric distress can either cause a desire for a mind-altering substance *or* the post-intoxication mental and emotional experience can spark symptoms of mental illness.

Unlike many categories of mental illness, which have only developed in the past hundred years, instances of substance abuse have long existed in the human historical record. The most obvious, in the context of the Bible, is alcohol. Throughout its pages we find a variety of experiences with intoxication and reactions to it. Abstinence was required of those who entered the tent of meeting in the wilderness;[1] alcohol could be used to lower someone's inhibitions against their will and use them for another's personal gain, as in the stories of Lot's daughters or of David, Uriah, and Bathsheba.[2] The writers of the proverbs frequently speak of the drinking of wine or of *shekar*—either translated "strong drink" or "beer," depending on interpretation—as a forerunner of suffering, poverty, and

foolishness.³ For the sages of Proverbs, abstinence, moderation, and strict self- and other discipline is what will provide
wisdom, health, and wealth. In the prophets, we find alcoholic
intoxication often used as a metaphor and example of the failure of God's people to remain faithful and just; *you have wine
at your feasts, but pay no attention to God; you are heroes in
drinking wine, and villains in taking bribes against the inno-
cent; you get your neighbors drunk just to see them naked.*⁴ The
results of intoxication, like staggered walking and vomiting,
are used as metaphors for the "intoxication" of idolatry and
allegiance to foreign powers.⁵

The testament letters from Paul and his contemporaries
join the writers of the proverbs in advocating for abstinence, though for distinctly different reasons. In Proverbs,
self-discipline would lead to personal success; in the epistles,
sobriety is directly connected with proof of the indwelling of
the Holy Spirit and the renunciation of past pagan sensuality;
sobriety is required of those who want to belong to the new
church or to lead it.⁶ But sobriety, at least for Paul, does not
mean complete abstinence. He speaks casually of the "cup"
used at the Lord's supper, which would have been by tradition a chalice of wine; he also recommends wine for Timothy's
stomach troubles.⁷ Paul is not being hypocritical; he is following in a long biblical tradition that understands alcohol both
as a dangerous substance when taken in excess, and as a drink
of celebration that can symbolize God's abundance.

The anonymous writer of Ecclesiastes, often assumed to be
David's son Solomon, contests the wisdom of Proverbs with
their own writings, offering not moderation and abstinence
but enjoyment of life. "Eat and drink, and take joy in your

work," the Teacher repeats.[8] One anonymous psalmist adds to the chorus of wisdom: "God, you made wine, to make our hearts glad!"[9] Even among the prophets, who have loathed leaders who focus more on their empty cups than the needs of their people, we find a recognition that wine is for celebration; feasts that embody the generosity of God have wine and milk that require no purchase.[10] In all this, of course, there is also Jesus, working a miracle not of physical healing or spiritual salvation but providing more wine when wedding guests are already drunk.[11] Jesus points out the hypocrisy in religious judgment against either abstinence or indulgence: "A glutton and a drunkard!" he calls himself, imitating those who held his celebratory and expansive nature against him.[12]

The whole of Scripture does not speak with a single voice on the morality of a single glass of wine. Nor does it attend to a plethora of other addictive tendencies we might observe in its people. We might read in the stories of David and his sons a familial pattern of addiction to sex, from David's taking of Bathsheba, to his son Amnon's rape of his half-sister Tamar, to Solomon's seven hundred wives and three hundred concubines. This is complicated, of course, by the myriad differences in how sex was understood in the multiple places and eras of the Bible, and how it functions today. In biblical times, women essentially functioned as political pawns and signs of status, not as autonomous subjects who had agency over their own bodies and history; we can absolutely state that the house of David had a pattern of sexual abuse, but we cannot declare unequivocally that it is sexual addiction.

As with all mental illness, it is dangerous to read back our modern understandings of addiction onto individuals in history whose inner lives and emotional growth we do not have access to. To claim that the pattern of sexual abuse in the house of David is unquestionably indicative of a sex addiction would be to misunderstand how addiction is experienced. At the same time, the sex work and pornographic industries of today can persist in treating people (of all genders) as objects and possessions rather than as participants in their own enjoyment, and it is that kind of objectification that turns a partner in sex into yet another "substance" for one individual's intoxication. In the face of addiction, as with many other mental illnesses, the Bible can reflect human patterns that exist to today, but the translation is rarely perfect.

Anyone who has walked with addiction knows this. Those of us who seek recovery or sobriety, through individual self-discipline or any number of programs available, know that it may not be as simple as setting a proverb as our phone background. We long for the prescription of a single Bible verse or a heartfelt prayer to deliver us from the turmoil of addiction, and yet for many of us, we have found no deliverance there, only amplified shame.

Al-Anon, the program for family and loved ones of alcoholics, is the place where I came to face my own addictions. Unlike AA and its sister programs (Narcotics Anonymous, Gamblers Anonymous, and so on), Al-Anon and Alateen function as auxiliary groups—we are there because of someone else's addiction. Just like those in AA, we confess the same inability to control alcohol—but for us, it's someone else's use. And yet, for some of us (myself very much included), we come to know that our turmoil in facing addiction in a loved one is directly related to addictive patterns of our own, including a desire to help that becomes so consuming that we lose our sense of self. Our focus is entirely on keeping the other person sober or safe. When this becomes an extended pattern, it is often termed *codependency*. (A fellow Al-Anoner once told me wryly: "They say we're not addicted to anything, but the truth is, we are. We're addicted to people.") The all-consuming nature of keeping an addict away from their substance or from the consequences of using it can produce the same kind of emotional and mental high that a substance can—anxiety about not having it, relief when it is found, a growing need for reassurance that mirrors increasing substance tolerance.

All of this, of course, is deeply complicated by messaging within our Christian culture, which offers two contradictory expectations: The addict should be able to stop on demand, and the support system should be gracious. Those of us who walk with addiction can cite chapter and verse where our vices are prohibited, and yet for many of us that is not enough to stop the cycle—in fact, the shame and judgment in knowing exactly how doomed we are can make the desire for and consumption of our particular substance even stronger. Yet for many Christian approaches to treating addiction, we begin at trying to shame, guilt, or damn the addict into being "better." At the same time, we expect the support system around the addict to be eternally forgiving. "It's an addiction," we remind the exhausted spouse. "They can't help it. Just forgive them," we offer to an overburdened friend, ignoring that they have compromised their own ability to flourish in order to support the addict. If someone is struggling with the burden of codependency, our attempt to help can actually encourage their continued self-neglect. With surface-level answers to problems of addiction, we can actually feed the addictions themselves.

Many of us in twelve-step programs know the dichotomy between the theology practiced in church basements over stale coffee and the theology preached and experienced in Sunday worship. For those of us where church has seemed like one more place where we need to have it all together, recovery programs can feel like a safe haven where we know everyone else is a mess too. With leadership roles constantly in rotation, we are treated as the experts on our own story, rather than deferring to authorities who have the qualifications to damn us if we step out of line. The halting language of each ordinary person trying to experience God as an active liberator from addiction in our individual lives can feel more eloquent than a finely crafted sermon. And at the end of each meeting there is the invitation: *take what you like, and leave the rest*, an acknowledgement that recovery is not identical and one person's experience is not universal.

But while popular church messaging might not be the only answer, AA might not be either. Many addicts struggle with the twelve steps (for whatever substance). Introductions at twelve-step meetings usually expect the person to say "My name is ____, and I'm an alcoholic," but this enforced labeling can be experienced as judgmental and as exacerbating for the addict: *Well, if I am one, might as well drink!* The admission of powerlessness, particularly within historically marginalized groups, can aggravate experiences of distress and self-hatred; rather than addressing a multitude of potential causes of addiction (including, often, systematic oppression, personal trauma, or cultural disempowerment), the structure of twelve-step groups make it an entirely personal event. The total abstinence expected in a majority of AA and NA home groups also makes it difficult to transfer into groups like Overeaters Anonymous; one can avoid interaction with opioids or narcotics, but not with food, and the teaching of "powerlessness" can contribute to binge eating or bulimia. And of course, the requirement of believing in a Higher Power sets back many people who come to self-help groups with a bad taste for religion already in their mouths. Twelve-step programs found their start in two men, a stockbroker and a surgeon, who found freedom from alcoholism in defining themselves as powerless and relying on the intervention of an evangelical Protestant understanding of God and the help of other addicts. This is not the experience of every person with addiction, and when it is treated as the only possible source of recovery, it can be detrimental.

Yet Christian faith has a multitude of gifts for approaching and walking with addiction, if we let it. We live in the frustrating tension between our capacity for choice and our need for a source of power outside ourselves; our lived experience shows that we have some authority over our actions, yet often choose what is detrimental to ourselves or others even when we "know better." We live in a long faith history of recognizing that, as individuals or as an interrelated society, we need some form of calling to repentance and transformation, some kind of grace for when we fail. A more expansive understanding of addiction, as not just a personal failing that a Bible verse can band-aid over but a complex system of biology, psychology, experience, and access, can open each of us, addict or not, to understanding the multitude of factors that go into our own lives and decisions. By better understanding ourselves, we might be better able to step out of negative coping mechanisms and into actions (and eventual habits) of care for ourselves and our neighbor.

A transformed understanding of addiction might also inform our thoughts and actions around transgression and forgiveness. In recovery programs, addicts are asked to take responsibility for their actions as they pursued or used their particular substance. Powerless or not, we are still culpable for what we did. In twelve-step programs, half of the program is focused on where we have harmed others and how we can make amends for it.[13] Can you imagine if half of every Christian worship service was dedicated to unflinching inventories of where each person had hurt someone else (themselves included) and how, exactly, they wanted to make it right? Not how we as a collective had all sinned and fallen short of the glory of God, through which we could only be delivered (but entirely would be!) by faith in Jesus—what if each person stopped and took stock of how they could fix what they had broken, and what they had to do to not do it again? (I suspect attendance would go down.) Our practiced and proclaimed faith would radically transform if we allowed ourselves to be brutally and humbly honest about what felt empty and unfulfilled and terrifying within us, and then refused the simple solutions offered by either substance use or surface-level faith. We are, perhaps, a little nervous about knowing ourselves that well, about peeling back the veneer of our Sunday best and putting away the coping mechanisms that allow us to pretend the shine is more than skin deep. But perhaps that kind of deep knowing—where we recognize who we are, and allow others to do the same—would be the beginning of an embodiment of the unending grace of God.

QUESTIONS TO ASK

As with all questions and accompaniment, these are best asked when a person is stable, not when they are intoxicated or hungover.

- How is [substance or behavior] getting in the way of who you want to be?
- How do you feel when you [use substance or behavior]? Is there a way to get that feeling without it?
- What are you afraid to face?
- Tell me about how you see God. *(Some of us who live with addiction have either a vision of a judgmental and condemning God, who we can never live up to, <u>or</u> a merciful and compassionate God who loves everyone . . . except us. Unweaving those threads can help start a new image of God that reflects wide mercy for everyone, ourselves included.)*
- Can you tell me a story about forgiveness? *(Many of us who live with addiction return to our substance because of our cycle of shame and guilt. Inviting us into imagining forgiveness—in stories of friends or family, or in the Bible—can sometimes unlock a belief that we, too, could be forgiven.)*
- What do you want the future to look like?
- What's working for you in not [using substance or behavior]? How can I / we support that?

- What are you grateful for today? *(Addiction can often arise in situations that feel hopeless. Practicing gratitude is one part of many recovery programs that seek to re-orient the mind toward positive parts of life rather than hyper-focus on the negative.)*

FURTHER READING

Martha Postlethwaite, *Addiction and Recovery: A Spiritual Pilgrimage*, Fortress Press, 2019.

Nadia Bolz-Weber, *Pastrix: The Cranky, Beautiful Faith of a Sinner & Saint*, Jericho Books, 2014.

On a rich fictional exploration of science, faith, and addiction: Yaa Gyasi, *Transcendent Kingdom*, Knopf, 2020.

CHAPTER TEN

SUICIDE

A content warning before we begin that I speak openly about the feelings of suicidal ideation that I and others have experienced. In keeping with current language recommendations by psychiatric resources, I use terms like "died by suicide" and "suicide attempt."

If you or someone you care about is currently experiencing serious suicidal ideation, please call a crisis hotline like the Suicide Prevention Lifeline at 800-273-8255 for immediate help.

What I remember most is the anger.

My twenty-eighth year had begun with a lot of hope. I was in a long-term relationship that I believed was headed toward marriage; I was finishing up the back half of my seminary education to become a pastor; I was in the beginning part of an internship at a local congregation under a supervisor that I thought was amazing.

Then everything just . . . broke.

The deep and sustaining friendships from the first two years of seminary were suddenly all distant as each of us launched onto an internship or graduated and moved into career work. My internship supervisor got a once-in-a-lifetime opportunity that she could not faithfully refuse, and so suddenly I had a new supervisor in charge of my program for the next eighteen months, while trying to walk with a congregation through saying goodbye to their beloved pastor. Shifting friendships and changing supervisors are not unusual or particularly destabilizing in themselves, but it meant that the world around me was already shifting. Then the relationship that had been my anchor for many years fell apart.

By a few months into age twenty-nine, I found myself living in a friend's basement on a borrowed air mattress with a few suitcases of clothes, out of which I rotated to make my way through my half-time at seminary and my half-time internship. The loneliness of close friends now distant, the shift in supervisors—these were disappointments, but certainly something I could handle. But the end of my first long-term relationship seemed to prove everything that I had been trying to avoid about the church's stereotypes of queer relationships. I felt like I had failed not only myself and the woman I had loved, but also every person struggling for a space within the church for recognition of their relationships. If I couldn't keep mine together, how could I promise anybody else that they could manage theirs? If I had been so certain of something in the past and now it wasn't true anymore, could I be really certain about my call to ministry, about my faith, about Jesus, about my sexuality, about anything? How could I ever be a pastor, ever be a girlfriend again if I had hurt someone I claimed to love so much?

I felt like a failure.

I felt like so much of what I had based my identity on was falling apart, crumbling out from beneath me after years of pressure of trying to fit myself into molds that other people would find acceptable and approvable. It turns out that no matter how hard you pack it, sand is still sand, and you can't build a house on it.

I was going to Al-Anon[1] at least once a week, along with regular therapy. I was doing okay in my classes and figuring out how to preach in the midst of feeling like everything I knew about myself was falling down. To be honest, I preached some of my best sermons that year; a lot of seeds can be sown in the soil of desperation, in the need for something to be real and in the willingness to speak about our brokenness. I was doing okay work, in classes and in church, and I had a support system in place. But in the midst of all that, everything felt hopeless.

I was lying in my friend's basement bathroom. The cool tile pressed against my back. I felt angry. Because there was nowhere I could go that I could die.

I didn't want to die in my friend's bathroom and have her find me. I didn't really have anywhere else to go. I certainly wasn't going to leave a note somewhere and then die in my car and make my parents and my friends and my church come find me.

I was so angry to be so loved.

I did not know how to go on. And I did not know how to not go on.

As someone training to be a pastor, suicide was not an unfamiliar concept. I had talked with people wrestling with suicidal ideation[2] and sat with families grieving after a loved one's death by suicide. But in those experiences, I found that my own journey with mental illness provided a much better framework than class lectures or textbooks ever had. In high school, a friend who knew my struggle with depression gave me a youth group craft project: a pop can, half-crushed and then spray painted, with careful permanent marker lettering: GOD MADE YOU AND GOD DON'T MAKE JUNK. The Christian church's response to suicide seemed as canned as that craft was: well-intentioned, but it could only hold so much water, and I was drowning. The promises of faith, the potential condemnation to Hell, the hope of resurrection and a new dawn every morning: None of that was finding me on that cool bathroom floor. All I had was anger at being so loved.

I reached for my phone, and for once I didn't text my ex. I texted a friend instead.

Hey, I typed, as casually as one can try to be when they are in the throes of desperation. *I'm having a tough day. Can you make sure I go to an Al-Anon meeting tonight?*

Sure, she replied, almost immediately. *Are you okay?*

There are so many ways to answer that question. No, I was definitely not feeling okay. At the same time, I was not in any physical danger.

I don't really want to talk about it. But there's a meeting tonight at 5:30, can you just check in with me at 5:00 and make sure I've gone?

Sure, she said.

And I made it to the meeting. And I made it to the next day. And the next. And the next, and the next. My world had shaken and the foundations had shifted, but love dug in deep and helped me find bedrock. And the next day came, and the day after that, and then one day I was thirty-three, and an ordained pastor, and marrying the love of my life. At my wedding, I danced with the friend who had texted back. She was nine months pregnant with her first son, and she had just finished the edits on my first book.[3]

I said that what I remember most was the anger, but what has endured was the love.

Suicide asks questions that few of us feel equipped to answer. *What is the purpose of life? How do we go on living when everything seems in despair? What does it mean that someone else could not go on living, even when those around them tried to show their love, compassion, grace, mercy? What does it mean when someone is gone and we do not know what has happened to them?*

There is very little discussion in the Bible of suicide. The Torah does not specifically outlaw it, though the Talmud expands teachings on murder and blood-spilling to include prohibitions on suicide. The majority of suicides in the Hebrew Bible are the result of failed military campaigns, when leaders or advisors recognized they were about to be taken captive; they chose to die at their own hands rather than in the disgrace of capture or the terror of torture and execution.[4] Some might argue that Samson dies by suicide in his destruction of the Philistine temple, since its toppling also kills him.[5] These are particular kinds of deaths for particular kinds of causes, and they are motivated very much by the military conquests happening in the historical books of the Hebrew Bible. They can be considered suicides in the technical sense, but to compare them to a majority of contemporary suicidal ideation and acts, we would have to neglect a lot of the story itself. In all these cases, as they are presented within the context of the Hebrew Bible, there is no reflection offered in the text itself as to the destiny of the souls of those who have died by suicide.

The New Testament brings a much more concrete understanding of a divided afterlife with rewards and punishments, but even there, suicide is not discussed as an act but rather presented as a reaction to events of great guilt or danger. In one such story, Paul and Silas have recently entered Macedonia, but have been jailed in the city of Philippi after exorcising a fortune-telling demon from a slave girl. A great earthquake shakes the prison, knocking all the cell doors open and the chains loose. The guard, certain that his prisoners have escaped, takes a sword to kill himself (likely as a preferable choice to the execution waiting for him for losing them), but Paul cries out to stop him, and the guard is not only spared from his own hand but converted to belief in Jesus.[6] As in the stories of the Hebrew Bible, the guard's suicidal ideation is most likely out of fear of his punishment.

Judas's death might be cited as a clear example of suicide outside of a military conquest or capital punishment for a crime, but even there the cause and end are unknown. In the Gospel of Matthew, Judas repents of his betrayal of Jesus and seeks to return the silver he was paid; when the religious leaders refuse to take it back, he throws it on the ground and leaves to hang himself. The religious leaders then use the silver to buy a field to bury unclaimed bodies; it is not specified if Judas will be one of them.[7] In the book of the Acts of the Apostles, however, *Judas* is the one who buys a field, and then has a serious fall, which causes his torso and stomach to burst.[8] In both stories, the field becomes known as *Akeldama*, "Field of Blood," but the purchase of the field and the death of the man who possessed the money are entirely different stories. In both versions, the shame cast on Judas is not about his manner of death, but on his betrayal of Jesus.

The suicides of Scripture, then, are not easily comparable to the multitude of suicidal ideations and actions today. Suicide within the context of mental illness is rarely directly connected to the failure of military conquest, although we should not neglect the psychological and emotional damage that military service induces; the 2019 National Veteran Suicide Prevention Annual Report found that the suicide rate for American military veterans was 1.5 times the rate of non-veteran adults, and that veterans make up 13.5 percent of all deaths by suicide in American adults but only 7.9 percent of the population. Even so, these suicides are not the same as suicides in biblical military history, as they occur not only while in service but also—in fact, well into the majority—occur when soldiers have been returned to civilian life.

Suicidal ideation, or at least something close to it, also occurs in holy Scripture. In the story of Jonah, the prophet's experiences are exaggerated to the point that many scholars think it is meant to serve as a cautionary tale rather than a historical recounting. In such hyperbolic fashion, Jonah has succeeded in his prophetic mission (already a hint that the story might not be historically perfect—prophets rarely have great success), but is furious that the town of Nineveh is now going to be spared. He sits down to sulk and watch, just in case, but then curses when a newly grown tree withers and takes away his shade. "Is it right for you to be angry about the tree?" says God. "Yes! Angry enough to *die!*" snaps back Jonah, in what again seems a little too exaggerated to be true.[9] Even so, God does not scold Jonah for his ideation (whether sarcastic or real), but for his unwillingness to accept the grace extended to the Ninevites.

Paul, too, expresses a desire for death. His is borne not of grief nor of frustration, but out of a longing for unity with Christ. In the letter to the church in Philipi, he writes: "My desire is to part and be with Christ, for that is far better; but to remain in the flesh is necessary for you."[10] Here again, we experience someone who would prefer death to life (and specifically for Paul, prefers the afterlife to life), but to categorize either Paul or Jonah as experiencing suicidal ideation might read more into what they say than is there.

The desperation and despair that distinguishes suicidal ideation is also present in scriptural stories of extreme grief. Job, faced with the violent death of all his children and painful sores all over his body, curses the day he was born.[11] The psalmists cry out in lament again and again, describing beds drenched in tears, pain borne in the soul, desolation and isolation.[12] In all of these cases—grief, anger, despair, or a longing for the life after this life—when a desire for death is discussed, there is no consequence or condemnation. To be so moved as to long for death is not proof of abandonment by God or some state of unrighteousness; Jesus himself quotes the psalmist when he asks, "My God, why have you forsaken me?"

There is very little discussion in the Bible of suicide, even less of suicides whose motivations parallel modern cases, and even less of what happens after such a death. The silence left by Scripture has been eagerly, and often traumatically, filled by Christians. Many of us who live with mental illness can tell the horror stories of funeral sermons or comments on a Facebook eulogy. We have heard, over and over, that suicide gives its initiator only one destination, that it is a waste of a God-given life, and that it can only lead to eternal damnation.

This is not a theology that I can ascribe to for several reasons—but it is a theology that I can understand. When we are faced, as pastors or as friends or loved ones or care-givers of any kind, with someone asking about the purpose of continuing to live when they have no will to do so, it is easy to run out of resources. We long to grasp onto something firm, something unquestionable, something that will keep the person unmoved even as they feel torn up inside; something that will keep them here until their hope, their love for life, their passions return. We are looking for any kind of foot-hold to keep us from falling off the mountain.

I sometimes envy pastors and churches that have a more condemning theology than I do. It feels far easier to influence behavior—to say to the addict, the bipolar, the suicidal patient that to engage in their behaviors is unquestionably wrong. I understand the draw of that kind of theology, because then the conversation is over. A Christian who speaks of the symptoms and behaviors of mental illness as something to be shamed and condemned puts any work or struggle back on the sufferer's shoulders. They deny any calling to carry the burden along-side me, no dealing with my addictions or wandering through the valley of my despair. Now they have left the burden on me. And beloveds, when I am tired, when I have nothing left to give, I can understand why someone would counsel me in this way. When I have been in those deep and damning places, I understand why others might have nothing to grab but only the promise of eternal condemnation. They are just trying to keep me alive, by any means necessary. If nothing else will convince me to stay, perhaps the promise that the next life would be even *worse* will.

Of course, the problem here (if there is only one problem) is that we cannot exactly flip the switch. We might desperately teach that "suicide will lead to your eternal damnation" in the hope that we might save a life, and then be forced at a funeral to confront what our teaching will now speak into the lives of grieving family and friends. It would be disingenuous to turn around and say "we cannot truly know what God might think." I have sat through sermons on suicides that have tried to caution the rest of us away from it. If we are too lax around suicide, if we treat it with too much grace, might we not encourage others to consider it, attempt it? I am loath, beloved, to even write this chapter, because I fear I will be too permissive. Am I too gentle? Should I speak only in the words of condemnation, so that no one will think that there is grace? Would it save a life, to lie and say I know God's will?

I think again of myself, lying on a friend's bathroom floor. And then I think of parents, partners, children, friends, loved ones that I have had to sit beside and try to explain where I think their loved one has gone. Where is love in preaching against suicide? Is it to condemn the suffering, in order to save? Is it to preach grace to the mourner, in order to salve?

Years ago, I stopped in at my job as a children's education director at a small church in South Minneapolis, to unload some recent craft store purchases and check our construction paper stock before Sunday. It was that night I discovered there was a local suicide survivor's group that met in the same basement on Tuesday nights as our classrooms did on Sunday mornings. They were as startled by me as I was by them, but they were not unaccustomed to being interrupted, and after I closed the door and backed out, I saw their entry on the week's schedule taped to the door.

It took me a few months to understand that suicide survivors were not people who had made non-fatal suicide attempts, but rather the people that suicide deaths left behind. I realized then that their work was as much hallowed ground—or even more—than what was done in the sanctuary on Sunday mornings. They were making their way through a valley of death, in a way that few (and I pray each day that fewer still) will ever come to know. I came to recognize that work as holy, and I made sure there were enough Kleenex boxes in the room before I left on Sundays.

I cannot tell you, if you are walking that valley in the shadow of someone else's death, where the path is going to take you. I can only tell you it is holy work, and that I will find you Kleenex, and you may make your home in the basement of the church for as long as you need until you have the strength (and only when you do, beloved) to take part in joy and laughter again.

Here is what I can tell you that I know of suicide.

There is not one reason. Perhaps for one individual there is one reason, but there is not one reason for the problem of suicide. There is not one reason that someone thinks of it; there is not one reason that people plan for it; there is not one reason that people attempt it; there is not one reason that some attempts are fatal and some are not.

You are not at fault. Many of those left behind after a completed suicide blame themselves: *If only I had done something different.* We question our actions and our conversations, wondering if there was something we missed, or if we could have returned a phone call earlier, or if the boundary we set was unfair. Others close to us, hopefully well-meaning, might ask prying questions that make us think we could have and should have done more. We are especially fraught if a suicide attempt occurs close to a life event that we had a hand in—after a breakup, for example. Walking with someone who has experienced suicidal ideation requires us to confess our own idolatry: We are not God, and we are not a savior. We cannot be everything to a person. To be asked or expected to be someone's sole source for existence is a burden too big for any human to carry for long. While we might be able to provide immediate support for someone in urgent danger, no single human can bear the sole purpose of another person's existence.

There are times, however, when suicidal ideation and attempts can and perhaps should be directly linked to the abusive systems under which a person suffered. The high rate of post-service suicides among veterans, for example, points to problems within a militant system, in which death is seen as a solution to a problem, and where mental health assistance is difficult to ask for and even harder to receive. Parental rejection of an LGBTQIA+ child is another, where lack of familial acceptance is correlated with double the number of suicidal thoughts or suicide attempts.[13] We cannot be someone's savior, but we also should never be their source of condemnation.

There are times when suicide is a confession: *I have tried everything and I see no hope*. There are times when suicide is a way of saying, *I cannot go on*. Confession, in the Christian tradition, is a radical act of truth-telling. Confessing the faith is a statement of belief in the impossibility of a triune God incarnate in human skin. Confessing our sins is a counter-cultural willingness to admit when we have failed, have wounded others, or are in need of help. Confession is a personal apocalypse, a peeling back of the layers we plaster on to make the truth pretty. There are times when suicide is a confession: *I am telling you the terrifying truth about my life*.

There are times when suicide is a cry for help: *I have tried to tell you how greatly I am suffering and you cannot hear me*. We sometimes think of these as cries for attention, as facetious and impulsive. I will certainly not deny that those exist. But to think that suicidal ideation or attempts are not serious, to roll our eyes at someone "asking for attention" as if they might not be asking for attention to a deep emotional wound gone gangrenous in their soul, is to put an incalculable number of lives in danger.

What we know of many suicides is that people experience regret. We know this from the stories of people who have been drawn back from jumping off cliffs, or rescued from the water beneath the Golden Gate Bridge. I know this from a story pressed out from a seventeen-year-old girl in a hospital bed, her stomach full of neutralizing charcoal: *Halfway through I realized I didn't really want to do this.* We know that regret is common. For many who have experienced non-fatal suicide attempts, here is a sudden realization. What seemed insurmountable, perhaps might actually be conquerable. What seemed like the end could perhaps just be a semicolon.

I want to acknowledge that there are stories in which **some people understand suicide as a gift they give themselves and others** when they feel their life has become untenable and unsustainable. For some people, it is the option of physician-assisted suicide, when progressive physical or mental illnesses make their life too difficult to continue and too much of an imposition on those around them. For too many, it is a misunderstanding, a believing of the lies of mental illness: "you are alone," "you are unloved," "you are unwanted." Too many have these lies come to too much fruition, where they believe the world would be better off without them, and if they stood at their funeral would know that it was not so.

I know that for some, **suicide was the answer where no other option for freedom existed**. For many in abusive situations, in neglectful families, in military or political or prison situations in which freedom was meaningless and existence was a never-ending cycle of trauma and abuse, there seemed no other escape. Many of us, mental illness or no, have known what it is like to imagine leaving our current life behind, and starting over in a brand-new city. For most of us, that fantasy fades quickly as simply an escapist daydream, and we return to the slings and arrows of our reality in which we still can find great joys. For those of us who wander a bit more down the daydream's path, we realize that to begin again would require a fake ID, a new social security number, the complete destruction of any support network that might accidentally leave a trail to where our problems (real or imagined) could find us again. And there are some who long for a new start to life but—because of physical or financial abuse, for example—have no such option. Consider the introduction of no-fault divorce in America; before no-fault, divorce required consent of both or proof of fault by the non-consenting spouse. In a longitudinal study, two researchers found that the introduction of no-fault divorce in the 1970s reduced women's suicide rates by 6 percent, with a nearly 20 percent decline in female suicides over the next twenty years.[14]

For some, suicide has seemed like the only option to escape otherwise devastating situations. And **sometimes suicidal ideations or attempts are momentary and fleeting**, are disconnected from reality in ways that the person experiencing them cannot begin to understand. This is why many of the people that I know that walk with mental illness, even if they believe in the rights of the Second Amendment or live in a situation in which they fear for their lives or their safety, do not keep guns in their house. The momentary feelings of suicidal ideation are too easily carried out if there is such a murderous weapon readily at hand.

When suicide is this complex, what do we do? Too long we have defaulted into the two common ditches of Christianity's approach to mental illness: We try to silence it, or in fear of making a mistake, we silence ourselves. Neither of these can carry water. An offhanded "God never gives you more than you can handle" ignores the cries of those whose burden has grown far too heavy to witness, much less bear; our silence, too, allows shallow platitudes to be the only source of wisdom, and they too quickly fail. If someone dear to us confesses their own heavy burden, we have tasks at hand.

Our first challenge is to recognize the suffering of the person before us (or, if we are the one suffering, to face our own pain). We are animals still, remember, and our instinct is to shy away from what hurts. We do not want to face our own lack of answers; we do not want to face our own questions and mortality; we do not want to do it wrong. But we are part of a faith whose primary symbol is a symbol of pain and torture. The cross at the heart of Christian life is a place where God weeps and dies. Perhaps one of the many ways to see the work of crucifixion in our faith is to witness God's suffering in the suffering of others. Perhaps the crosses in our churches and homes are meant to be a reminder: *We do not have to be afraid of pain. God went into it first.* If, when someone shares their struggle, we can react with openness and compassion rather than anxiety and urgency, we can embody a rejection of the impulse that their current feeling needs an immediate reaction.

When someone shares their struggle—or when our own struggle becomes too much to hide even from ourselves— perhaps we are called not to turn away from the conversation but to sit, and be still, and compassionately listen. Too often we may want to rush to answers, finding promises that there is a reason to go on. This is not a bad impulse—it is only sometimes too quick. If suicide is the language of confession and a cry for help, then when we are invited into it, perhaps we are invited to listen with compassion and curiosity, to ask questions not to try to lead them somewhere but to let there be enough space for truth and hope to enter in. We may think we are offering the gift of our own advice, but the more space we can allow for a suffering person to find their own path to hope, the more firmly that path will be laid.

As you ask questions, you can summarize or paraphrase what the person is saying (without just parroting their words, of course!) to show that you're absorbing what is being said and thinking deeply about it.

But still, we are called to remember that we are never someone's sole source for survival. Suicide is most often an isolating experience, and entering into someone else's suffering can be too. We do not have to provide all the answers, or even all the emotional support. We are asked, when faced with someone else's pain, to recognize what is ours to do. If we, for whatever reason—our own mental wellness, our limited energy, our frustrations—cannot provide support, or if an emergency situation is becoming apparent, we can point to other sources:

Suicide Hotlines: For many people, access to a nonjudgmental stranger who simply wants to listen and redirect their feelings away from hurting themselves is a life-saving event. Suicide hotlines, now available by text and chat as well as phone, can make an incredible difference in an emergency situation. It is important to note that many of these are staffed by volunteers and are temporary solutions, not a long-term treatment for the underlying mental health issues that may have been present before the suicidal ideation.

Emergency Services: Most suicide prevention resources strongly recommend calling emergency medical assistance (in the US, 911) if a person is considered a serious danger to themselves. The difficulty here, of course, is that emergency services can also sometimes aggravate an urgent situation, especially in mental health crises, and even more complicated if issues of race are at play. I invite you to put away this book for a moment and Google what crisis services might be available in your area—even if you don't bookmark the search right now, you'll be more likely to remember the options later when you might need them.

Distraction and Redirection: Because suicidal intent can be a momentary reaction to a situation, one practice in suicide prevention is to move the energy and focus away from the immediate situation. Some suggestions can be to take a walk or watch a favorite movie. If you are physically with someone who is experiencing suicidal ideation, you can invite them to go somewhere with you, even if it's as frivolous as a drive-thru late-night snack.

Therapy and Support Groups: For many who experience suicidal ideation, there are underlying mental health issues that may need to be addressed. At the same time, therapy or support groups can have hurdles—cost, time, access, capability. It's okay to check in with someone after a week or two and ask what kind of long-term support they might be able to build.

National Suicide Prevention Lifeline: 800-273-8255

QUESTIONS TO ASK SOMEONE
EXPERIENCING SUICIDAL IDEATION

- Tell me about what's going on.
- It's okay if you don't want to talk—I just want to understand, so say as much or as little as you like.
- What ways do you think of killing yourself? *(This is what is called a "risk assessment" question—is the person still in an ideation stage, or is there enough of a plan that intervention is needed to protect their life?)*
- You've told me you're thinking about [using x to hurt yourself]. Can you put it away so we can talk? Can you go into another room so you/we can't see it?
- *Asking open-ended* ("How do you feel?") *questions versus closed-ended* ("Are you sad or mad?") *ones.*
- What can I do to help?

FURTHER READING

On those mourning after a death by suicide: Ronald Rolheiser, *Bruised And Wounded: Struggling To Understand Suicide*, Paraclete Press, 2017.

On life after a non-fatal suicide attempt: Liz Petrone, *The Price of Admission: Embracing a Life of Grief and Joy*, Broadleaf Books, 2020.

IF YOU ARE EXPERIENCING SUICIDAL IDEATION:

Take a few deep breaths. You do not have to take any action on your thoughts right now. Find space between your thoughts and your actions. Your feelings of despair are real and serious, *and* they also do not need to be acted on immediately.

Make your space safe. Move into a space without access to substances or things that you could use to hurt yourself. You might be able to go for a walk, or simply move into another room. This isn't a permanent change—you're just moving for a while.

Find someone you can trust and who can be there for you. This might be a family member, friend, therapist, pastor, teacher, family doctor, or coach—someone who knows you and can sit with you, either in person or at a distance. If you don't feel like you know someone who can be there for you right now, an experienced counselor at the end of a helpline can also be a resource. If the first person you reach out to doesn't understand or can't be present for you right now, that's okay—it is a normal human thing to not be available 24/7, and is not a judgment on you. Try someone else.

Share what's going on. Many of us who have experienced suicidal ideation know it can feel shameful or scary to be honest about what's happening inside our heads, but we also know it can be a huge relief to start talking about where we are emotionally and how we got there.

*   *   *

Keep breathing. A lot of people have gone through this and have made it to the other side. You may feel alone, but you are not the first person to experience this, and you can get through it, even if that seems impossible right now. Take time with yourself, and don't act like you have to go through these feelings alone.

Change is a constant—and so is love. Our situations change, our feelings change, the people around us change. Small changes today—or just holding on until something around us changes—can be the start of incredible changes in the future. No matter where you are, there is love waiting for you when you are ready.

CHAPTER ELEVEN
BOUNDARIES

"Pronouns? What's that?"

I glanced up. I'd just laid out the nametags and sign welcoming people to our monthly Queer Grace Community worship, an evening gathering of LGBTQIA+ Christians, faith-curious, and church-adjacent people in the Twin Cities. We launched in 2017, a collective of longtime Lutherans and ecumenical mutts and post-evangelicals seeking some form of religious community that didn't expect us to check our identities and our lives at the door. We are spiritually undisciplined, with histories of theological abuse from churches and church leaders that sought to dictate our existence and actions, yet longing for the kind of structure and community that former churches offered. We are hungry for the bread of Jesus and sick of being given stones instead. And so we gather, in the elementary school turned community center that Grace Lutheran Church launched or in an old warehouse turned into art studios and a coffee shop, and we try to figure out what we do with this gift and burden we call faith.

Nametags with pronouns are an essential part of our life together; it allows everyone, no matter their gender identity, to move within the space without assumptions based on appearance. Cisgender attendees, whose gender identity is the same as the sex they were assigned at birth, display their pronouns right alongside trans and nonbinary people, whose gender identities differ from their assigned sex. Genderqueer and genderfluid people can adjust their pronouns week to week. No one had questioned the move when we'd started it, but now two strangers who didn't seem to know each other but had come in at the same time were staring at the sign and the stickers in very different ways. It's not unusual for people to not have seen pronouns before, although I'm surprised when LGBTQIA+ people under forty haven't.

"It means you put your pronouns under your name?" guessed the second stranger, gesturing at the handmade sign. "Like she and her or him and his or whatever."

"Well, that's—" Here the first stranger used the r-word.

Everyone in the room froze. The worship band, milling around and making copies of sheet music in the last few minutes before we officially started, glanced at me with stunned silence. I blinked, similarly shocked.

The queer and faithful community is a messy place. We come with painfully heavy baggage. A majority of those who show up have stories to tell of expulsion from home churches, colleges, families, friend groups, seminaries, and pulpits. Most of us have come to the Queer Grace Community with the hope of church finally acting like One Big Happy Family. You know the kind—where everyone's personal and professional desires line up smoothly with others, where we all just play Pictionary and laugh until we cry into our perfectly crimped pumpkin pie. We don't have to discuss politics, because everyone agrees. Conversations around needs, wants, and consent don't happen, because we automatically know and respect each other's exact dimensions of comfort. This hope is not blithe; it comes from often long histories of having to negotiate painful conversations with unaffirming family of origin and condemning home pastors and congregations. We have had to shake off the confining, even traumatic, expectations of loved ones. We are weary of the lines we have had to draw, and we would like to just be welcome, no strings attached, no bar to clear. For a long time, this is where my understanding of the kingdom of God rested: a place where everyone was welcome without exceptions, because we were all too familiar with what happens when a church draws a line in the sand.

The shift for me came in witnessing to the work of anti-racist activists like Elle Dowd, sexual abuse survivors like Emily Joy, and disability advocates like Shannon Dingle. It came in diversifying my Twitter timeline beyond the people in my Contacts list and my bookshelf beyond the required reading for seminary. In observing advocacy work, I saw lines again drawn, but this time not to damn those on the outside but to protect those on the inside. There were expectations for behavior: repentance and atonement for the sins of the past, commitment to eliminate those abuses in the future. The survivor of assault is not seated next to her rapist. We do not give equal time to those crying out for Black lives to matter and those who carry flags meant to intimidate and silence. Victim and abuser cannot sit at the same table. This is not a line that supports the societal expectations and personal comforts of those in power; this is a line that disrupts the systems that perpetuate violence and abuse.

From that jumbled library of my mind, I tried to decide what to do next. Perhaps this stranger did not know that the r-word is a slur. Perhaps they were confused as to the shape of the community that was gathering. Perhaps they were dangerous and had come deliberately to be hurtful to our community. I had only a few minutes before I needed to start worship. Should I delay our start time and pull them aside for a conversation? Should I tell them in front of the whole group "That language isn't welcome here," so that everyone would know they were protected from further slurs? Should I ignore it, out of compassion for their own potential journey? This is the calculus of community: How do we have expectations, without hindering love?

This mental math is particularly crucial in the journey of mental illness, where boundaries are essential for the health and wholeness of both the person living with mental illness and for the people around them. Those of us living with mental illness need to understand the limits of our own emotional capacities, or we find ourselves overextended and more likely to use negative coping mechanisms or fall into toxic thought patterns. It is difficult, when we ourselves have borne the baggage of unrelenting anxiety, not to empathetically accompany someone else who is experiencing the same thought cycles—and yet if we do so, it is much more likely that our own anxiety will be triggered. Many of us with mental illness want to help others, especially when their symptoms are well-known to us, and yet when we do so, we endanger our own health and healing.

In a similar way, the people who love and accompany those living with mental illness can easily find themselves overextended and resentful, because our own behaviors and emotional needs can quickly become overwhelming when boundaries are unestablished or disrespected. Friends, family, the church community might feel taken advantage of by mounting emotional demands, yet fear that saying "no" would put a person in greater distress. In our haste to support or advise, we might find ourselves inadvertently enabling symptoms, because we provide care without empowering an individual to sustain themselves. Making the first therapy appointment for someone stalled by anxiety can be a gift; driving them to every appointment for the next six months quickly creates a cycle of dependency.

No conversation around boundaries can ignore when they are violated to the point of manipulation or abuse. Those of us living with mental illness are not in a special category that either amplifies a tendency to be abusive nor excuses manipulative behaviors, yet both are often assumed. We might be expected to be particularly ill-equipped to be in relationships (romantic, familial, friendly, or otherwise) because we cannot handle our own feelings; we might be, conversely, allowed to behave however we like because we "can't help it." Neither is correct, and neither helps us nor those who love us to create sustainable self-reflection and responsibility.

This is, of course, particularly complex within Christian practice, where we receive what seems like contradictory messages about God's unconditional love and about expectations for our own behavior. In some contexts, we are taught that everything is permissible as long as it spreads the gospel—for example, in the colonization, forced conversion, and/or genocide of non-Christian cultures and countries. In other contexts, we might be taught that expectations for our behavior are startlingly narrow; drinking, smoking, gambling, dancing, swearing all put our sanctification in mortal peril. Sex is also dangerous, unless it's within a church-sanctioned marriage, in which case it must be frequent enough to satisfy the man's desires and timed well enough to bear children. We bear in Christian history and contemporary practice an aggressive seesaw of law and grace, rarely with attention paid to those who are crushed in the cycle.

"Cancel culture" may be a new phrase, but shaming, condemning, and excluding people for their behavior is by no means a new practice. Yet shedding all expectations, in the hope of preaching a wide welcome and affirmation, puts individuals and the community in danger of violation.

Jesus himself drew lines. In his final sermon, he did not set at his right hand those who believed rightly, or did what the church leaders said to do. He did not prioritize those who could perfectly explain trinitarian perichoresis nor those who had properly maintained their assigned gender roles. He took those who wasted what they had on the least of the world: who fed the hungry, welcomed the stranger, visited the prisoner. And those on the other side of the line were not the doubters and stumblers, but those who had encountered a fellow human being in need and refused to meet that need. It was not that they had failed to recognize him, for so had those at his right hand; it was that they left the thirsty parched, the naked unclothed, the sick uncared for. The failure to recognize Jesus among the poor and needy was not the crime; it was the failure to recognize that each of us as we are, not because of the *imago Dei* but because of our precious humanity, are worthy of kindness.[1]

In his final sermon, Jesus himself drew lines. He told a ludicrous story of three servants (likely in such a position because of their own debts) given impossibly large sums of wealth to tend while their lord was away: five talents, two talents, one talent.[2] This is a story Christians tread well, especially come stewardship season, but the name of the coin has often given me pause: a literal translation of the Greek *talenton*, which began as money and came to be known as our inclination and desire for something. A talent, the notes in our study Bibles might remind us, was worth more than fifteen years' wages of a laborer. If we assume a forty-hour workweek and a living wage, we'd be looking at a single coin worth more than $150,000. No CEO would ever be so foolish as to take off for foreign lands and leave even the most responsible janitor in charge of their three-quarter-million 401(k). But the lord does, and when he returns, he finds that two servants traded and grew the wealth until it doubled—but the one given the least (yet still an impossible fortune) refused to use it. "You were just going to steal it like you've done everything else!" the servant shouts. The lord shakes his head: "Yes. That's the whole deal."

It's my own bias to assume that Jesus as the lord of the land is a good man, and that the story is meant to tell us something good. The world around us is full of immeasurable wealth: rare metals and precious gems, towering trees, rushing clear water, the air we breathe. We could not live without the world, and yet it is not ours, no matter how we might treat it. Humanity has dramatically shifted the globe and its climate since the Industrial Revolution, to a point at which we stand on the precipice of destruction, acting as if we can jump off the cliff and trust capitalism to build us a spaceship to a colonized Mars on the way down. This is what happens when we think wealth (from a billionaire's money to the abundance of natural resources) is ours; bubbles burst and stocks drop, and the earth will crumble under our feet if we beat it enough. What we have is not actually ours, not in the end. What we'll have is the legacy we leave for those who stand beside and come after us.

So the lord of the land chuckles: "The land is mine, and you work it, but the food it produces can feed far more than us four. The wealth is mine, and you had charge over it, but at the end of days everything will be revealed as belonging to me. If you were unwilling to do the work, to tend what was given you, to prepare for how it could be expanded so that many would benefit, then give it to someone else! But you would not. I gave you unimaginable wealth, but you could not even spare a thought for how to use it."

In his final sermon, Jesus himself drew lines. He cast a dramatic rendition of the worst wedding reception in history, with five young women who came prepared and five who showed up wanting half the credit.[3] "Give us some of *your* oil," they demand of the women who showed up ready. "Then we'll *all* be in darkness," the early birds reply. "None of us will make it." I think of the summer of 2020, when white women showed up en digital masse to book clubs and Instagram posts about systemic racism, only for November to reveal that 55 percent of us would vote for Trump anyway. "Share your trauma," we demanded of Black Americans, retweeting the video of George Floyd crying for his mother as his breath labored under the suffocating weight of Derek Chauvin's knee. *Look how woke I thought we were*, I thought in early November, when it seemed like we'd all fallen asleep again. How long do I get to demand the emotional labor of others? How long do I get to show up unprepared and expect someone else to have done the work for me?

What I began to wonder was, if when God drew lines, they were not expectations but rather boundaries. Boundaries are a way of distinguishing two things from each other—in this case, people. At some point, you end and I begin. Boundaries are limits, not because I do not love the other person, but because my love for them does not transcend my own needs and values. Healthy boundaries keep me emotionally, mentally, and physically stable, establishing an identity that isn't based on what I can or will do for others. They allow me to refill my own energies and passions and to preserve my sense of self and my values. Boundaries, in short, are a way of speaking a holy and loving No.

Boundaries are not universal rules. Public displays of affection that are fun and welcome in one relationship might, for an equally happy other couple, feel awkward and self-conscious. Some boundaries can feel intrinsic to who we are; I have, since childhood, been a natural introvert who needs time alone to recharge and refocus. Other boundaries may be developed as a response to experience, even trauma; consider, perhaps, the partner who is not comfortable sharing their phone passcode because their ex would snoop on their phone for hours look-ing for nonexistent proof of infidelity.

But boundaries are not limited to romantic relation-ships; we make them with family, friends, and coworkers too. We create boundaries all the time, usually without knowing it—preferring to go home rather than out to happy hour, for example. Some boundaries may change over time; a child who doesn't mind hugging extended family at age six may, at age nine, no longer feel comfortable with close physical contact with people who feel like strangers. Most of us may not realize where our boundaries are until they have been crossed, inten-tionally or unintentionally. We feel uncomfortable, unsettled. Our stomach might turn upside down, or skin flush with anx-ious sweat. We want to escape the situation, but often can't, at least not right away. We may be confused: "Why am I feeling like this? What's wrong with me?" Only later, sometimes in self-reflection and sometimes over drinks with friends, are we able to put words to what happened.

In the age of social media, boundaries have become even more complex to navigate. Life used to be more cleanly divided into groups of people, but now, our distant cousin and a high-school classmate and a current coworker can all come together on Instagram to coo over a new puppy picture or scream in all caps about politics. The intimacy of social media, where everyone who can find us is invited into our homes, can feed situations of boundary-crossing that would have been much harder to activate when there wasn't a way for that guy whose request for our phone number at the coffee shop hadn't figured out where we worked, stalked the company Facebook page, found us tagged in a photo, and messaged us with very specific details about the depth of his desire for us.[4] He sees no violation of a boundary; after all, isn't it romantic he went to such an extent? There is no societal rule that says what he did was wrong; there are plenty of movies that suggest he is now the main character, demonstrating his passion and persistence and therefore attractiveness. And yet, many such attempts are unwanted, and trigger a series of conversations where we, the object of his affection, must artfully dodge the situation in fear he'll just start coming into our Starbucks every day and wear us down.

Boundaries are an essential part of healthy self-awareness and identity formation, but they require a sense of the self that a good portion of us (and a very large portion of those of us assigned and socialized female) are not taught. We are taught to be helpful, self-sacrificing, and other-serving. Movies that center on a lead female character are, no matter what their technical genre, chick flicks. We're taught how to load the dishwasher correctly, how to keep the five family calendars in balance, where the extra lunchboxes are stored in case a kid forgot one at school. We play supporting characters, both on screen and in our lives. To establish boundaries as someone socialized female, to say, "Here is where you end and I start," is consistently counter-cultural.

This enforced self-sacrifice for women and people socialized female particularly comes to play in Christian culture. Women were created second and therefore are to be helpers and servants. They cannot preach, they cannot teach. Despite women making up 50 percent of the population and 20 percent of seminary students, only 12 percent of American churches have senior or solo female pastors (the number jumps to 24 percent for mainline Protestants and crashes to 9 percent for evangelical churches).[5] Simply put, we are not viewed as leaders; we are support staff, and it is dangerous to the institution when support staff try to have boundaries. Boundaries are, at heart, a distinction between one person's needs and another person's wants, and those of us who are on the opposite side of a newly laid boundary have a great deal of trouble separating the two. It is much easier to try to find our way around these new and unfair "rules," to figure out how to still get what we want, than to reflect compassionately on why the other person needs to draw this line for their own health and well-being.

Not lending your car to a family member who's wrecked theirs means that they must feel the consequences of their choices—and most of us don't like to do that. We whine "but familyyy," and we get aunts in on the group text to shame the person who just wants to keep their working car in decent condition. Because boundaries are often realized only after they are crossed, it can feel like an unjust game of "take-backsies": "But you let me do _____ before!" Sometimes a boundary is laid only after several of the same instances, when we realize we can't keep ignoring our own reactions and needs. People who finally voice a boundary after multiple previous violations might be accused of bringing up the past, of failing to forgive and forget, when what is actually happening is not rehashing history but revealing a pattern.

Christian culture, for a multitude of reasons, has shied away from dealing with history. We prefer to teach endless second chances for those who hurt another. The burden is on the victim to excuse the actions of the abuser. After all, does not God have such grace with us, that we are such sinners and yet forgiven? But pull on the threads that make up this tapestry of "forgive and forget," and the knots unravel quickly. The institutional church has failed, over and over, to own up to its own sins in history: its happy cooperation with the violence of any empire that would claim allegiance to Jesus as long as they could kill for it; the genocide of Indigenous peoples who would not submit to forced baptism; the demonization of enslaved people and their descendants up through the end of segregation, at which point the church pivoted to abortion, away from cross-town school bussing, as its galvanizing political issue. We silence victims of clergy abuse; we romanticize the youth minister who patiently waits until the teenager turns eighteen to ask her father for her hand in marriage.

Most of the attendees of our little queer-and-Christian-ish gathering know their need for boundaries. When all eyes turned to me that Sunday evening, with the r-word slur echoing in our gathering space, I did not see shock, but weary experience. We know what it's like to be told "so-and-so just doesn't know any better" or "that's just how their generation is" or "you're being too sensitive." We've had to draw lines between us and abusive theology, condemnatory church leaders, vitriolic family. Those boundaries are often seen as rejection and a fracture of the relationship, but what they actually are (for the most part) is a way to *protect* the relationship and stay in it. We often have opted for porous boundaries, where we can still see extended family at Christmas with the established understanding that we'll leave the minute they start using deadnames. Boundaries, for us and for many, are a way of staying in relationship, rather than having to break it completely. Boundaries—like pulling someone aside to say, "We don't talk like that here"—mean that we don't spend the rest of an evening or the whole of a relationship on high alert, wondering when the next hurtful statement or action will come.

But personal boundaries are dangerous for the Christian church; it means we can no longer manipulate our members into total self-sacrifice for the benefit of the institution. And yet Jesus himself drew lines. When the disciples came asking, "But who is the greatest in the kingdom of heaven?" Jesus did not offer their hoped-for answer of "You righteous students of mine, of course!" but rather began a sermon on the importance of how we treat the least protected. Hurt a child? Millstone around the neck. Sinning with your eye or hand? Cut it off. Hold on to your desire to use and abuse others? Pit of fire.[6] Jesus has no patience for perpetual accommodations for those who violate the bodies and souls of others. There are boundaries in the kingdom of heaven, and they are drawn to protect children and the oppressed.

When those boundaries are violated, Jesus goes on to offer, there is still recourse. First, speak to the person who hurt you in private, where they can listen. If they do not listen, try again and bring one or two people with you, who can witness your hurt and their reaction. If they still will not listen, tell the whole assembly of the faithful, and if they still will not listen, that is the end of their relationship with the community.[7]

Can you imagine if we listened like that to the testimony of victims?

Can you imagine if we listened like that to the stories of Black, brown, Indigenous, and people of color?

Can you imagine if we listened like that to the worn-out volunteer who does not want to be asked to lead one more committee?

Hold up, I can hear some saying, *Jesus goes right on to say that if someone sins, we should forgive them, as much as seventy times seven. Forgive us our sins as we forgive others! To hold a little debt against someone when we have been forgiven an unimaginably massive one is cruelty worthy of torture.*[8] True! Jesus knew from the start that none of us, not even his closest disciples, would be perfect. We would cross boundaries, we would hurt another person, we would sin in the same old well-worn ways again and again. We would need forgiveness, from God and from each other, and we would need to learn to forgive. But simply because perfection before the kingdom has fully come is impossible does not make all behavior permissible, nor should we exist without guidelines for conduct within our community. Much of Paul's writings, to communities that were already convicted by the story of Jesus and empowered by the presence of the Holy Spirit, were about right behavior and right relationship.

Forgiveness, in the Judaism of Jesus's time and in the early church, was never about saying, "Ah, it's fine! Let's act as if it never happened!" It was not lending money to a debtor over and over again, pretending there was no history of unpaid debts before. Forgiveness was a recognition that the debt would not be paid. But reconciliation, the restoration of a relationship, cannot happen if the debtor refuses to recognize the grace they have been given or refuses to make conscious and continual attempts to show they are worthy of trust again. A debtor, a manipulator, an abuser cannot demand forgiveness if they will not recognize they have done wrong. A debtor, a manipulator, an abuser cannot demand forgiveness that allows them to hurt again with no consequences. Forgiveness is fruitless if the debtor has one hand over their heart to proclaim a false innocence and the other in our pockets stealing yet again.

This is where boundaries play an essential role: the restraint they provide offers a space for the relationship to exist and for trust to rebuild while the parties remain protected. Boundaries enable forgiveness. They negate requirements for eternal self-sacrifice for the benefit of another who is not sharing in that same self-giving. They allow us to maintain our internal sense of self. They reflect an understanding of each human being as *imago Dei*, made in the image of God, worthy of respect and preservation. They reiterate the boundaries that God has cast for right relationship, in which mistakes and forgiveness are expected but are, as best we can, repented, amended, and avoided. Boundaries are certainly essential for navigating the complicated emotional and behavioral symptoms of mental illness, but when understood as a gift and a balancing act, they serve not just those of us within particular DSM-IV categories but the whole body of Christ, allowing us to remain in precious and compassionate relationship with each other even as we beautifully differ in our needs and our gifts.

QUESTIONS TO ASK

- How can you tell when your boundaries have been crossed? What physical, emotional, mental reactions do you have?
- When do you cross your own boundaries? Why?

- When have you crossed another person's boundary? What happened?
- Name something in your life—a person, a habit, a chore or work task—that consistently frustrates, drains, or dehumanizes you. What is your usual response, and how well does that work? Is there a different way to draw a boundary with that life-draining thing?
- What kind of boundaries make it possible for you to be part of a community? What are some expectations (spoken or unspoken) among close friends, for example, that put you at ease when you are with them?
- What would it look like to have an experience of God or of spiritual community that had the kinds of boundaries your friend group has?

FURTHER READING

On boundaries: Anna Katherine, *Boundaries: Where You End and I Begin*, Hazelden Publishing, 1994.

On communicating boundaries: Marshall Rosenberg, *Nonviolent Communication (A Language of Life)*, Puddle Dancer Press, 2015.

On Christian boundaries: April Yamasaki, *Four Gifts: Seeking Self-care for Heart, Soul, Mind, and Strength*, Herald Press, 2018.

CHAPTER TWELVE
SELF-CARE

Come to me, all who are weary and carrying heavy burdens, and I will give you rest . . .

The problem is I rarely want rest.

I want productivity. I want success. I want to be the shiny penny. I want my life to go as smoothly as my Instagram stories suggest. I want to be right and good. I want to be welcoming without being overbearing and I want to have boundaries without ever having to say, "no." I want the energy to finish the next chapter and the next sermon and the next house project and still have plenty left for a jaunty walk around the lake that perfectly exhausts our poodle-Shih Tzu mix so she stops barking at literally everything that moves while I—oh, right, need a little more energy for that podcast recording.

. . . for I am gentle in heart . . .

I don't want to learn from humility. I want an influencer who can teach me the top ten ways to perfectly curate my social media so that I'm just aware enough of the world to never be out of the loop but just distant enough to never be overwhelmed by it. I want to talk about trauma, but with only a single tear gently tracing the line of my cheek without disturbing whatever is currently on trend in eye makeup. I wanna work hard and play hard and never get hurt (or at least never feel it).

. . . and you will find rest for your souls.

I don't want to be grouped in with everyone else. I want a little knot of friends who celebrate my successes and never have to worry about my nonexistent failures, who cheer me on in every venture and never bring up how badly I've misdirected myself in the past. I want people who love me but never have to speak truth in love. I don't want to be in some collective with everyone else who's struggling to stand. I don't want to have to pay attention to how my own drive and desires can run roughshod over the neighbor beside the road.

Of course, Jesus didn't ask what I want. Jesus just asked if I was weary.

And beloveds, I am. I am weary of a body that does not absorb its neurotransmitters on the normal schedule. I am weary of a mind that learned too early to spin fast. I am weary of a heart trying to be wide and getting eaten up in the process. I am weary of a world that just tells me to try harder or to shut up. I know that some of my burden is basic chemistry, best rewired with medication and green smoothies and walks in the sunshine. I know that some of my burden is the broken record of messages I know aren't true but tell myself anyway. And I also know that some of my burden is my own weary hand still clinging to the heavy yoke, saying to Jesus, "But it's my emotional support coping mechanism." I struggle to let go of the yoke I know, even though my back is breaking, because it's the burden I grew my knotted shoulders around. I know you're supposed to be easier, Jesus, but when has something new ever been that easy?

Those of us who live with mental illness—I think perhaps most of us who are human—know what it's like to mold our beautiful self to fit a less-than-beautiful situation. We fear criticism, so we talk worse about ourselves first. Our bodies are tense with unspoken frustration at work, so we're irritable with our loved ones at home. We stay up too late trying to relax and get up too early to fill ourselves with coffee. We're afraid to face who we are, so we date terrible matches in the hope we can become someone new. This is the burden we know, and it's got to be better than the burden we don't.

Doesn't it?

I've come to know, and daily keep coming to know, the complex interlocking of experience and response. I am not responsible for the genetics or thought patterns that built up my less-than-ideal brain chemistry; I did the best I could with what I had. I am not responsible for the situations I found myself in: growing up in a world still laden with sexism, coming out in a church still tainted with queerphobia, a sensitive only child in a family that tried to love each other well. I did the best I could with what I had. We who live with mental illness are not responsible for everything that happened to us, whether it was major and repeated trauma or the slow wearing of a drop of water on stone. In many cases, we cannot just think ourselves better or flip the switch from sick to healthy, not with all that happened before this day.

We are not responsible for everything that happened to us—but we are responsible for what we do with it. We are not gifted a hall pass for every time our broken pieces tear at the strength of others. Much as I want to, I cannot wield my depression as a defense against critique. My own rough history is not the only author of my present script, and she does not get to say how everyone else will act. If, in the rarest of cases, a long marital discussion reveals the past ten minutes of tension were due to my anxiety masterfully misinterpreting the situation, I do not get to keep letting it spin. Hurt people hurt people hurt people. If I let my hurt tell today's story, then tomorrow's will be told by those I hurt in the process. I am not responsible for what has happened to me, even what is still happening in my brain, but I am responsible for what I choose to do with it. Each day, I have the task of releasing the yoke I know too well and trusting that a new one can be lighter.

I try to release the yoke of expectation, and learn to bear gentleness. My future wife, then a girlfriend of less than a year, once challenged me to consider if I was a perfectionist. I replied, with full sincerity, "I couldn't be a perfectionist. I've never done anything even close to perfect in my entire life." I am not particularly patient with my own humanness. The moment I've identified a problem, I expect to live immediately into the solution. I've discovered (though I'll probably pretend otherwise tomorrow) this is not how being human works. Change takes time. The toxic mind patterns and negative coping mechanisms I've developed didn't happen overnight, and neither will choosing something new. Coping mechanisms that served me well, even saved me, five years ago may suffocate me now. Unweaving what I've learned and how I've acted takes time, and heaping judgment on myself for the speed at which I heal has mostly just slowed it down more.

For some of us who live with mental illness, this can look like finding the grace to do only one thing. Some of us have known what it's like to be so drained that getting out of bed feels like lifting a thousand-pound weight. Some days, the best we can do is just get through. For those who love us, and for us trying to love ourselves, some days "our best" looks so close to failure that we mistake the two. "You couldn't even shower?" we say to ourselves, searing with the scalding that only the voice inside our own heads can speak. "Did you eat at all today?" our loved ones ask, the attempt at kindness curdling with exhaustion. (We are not trying to hurt each other. We're just hurting from the trying.) Some days, the best we can do is not get worse. Some days, the best we can do is brush our teeth and leave the bed for the couch. It looks awful, and it feels awful, and the more I beat myself up for it, the slower I'll rise the next day. Bearing gentleness looks like tenderness with myself, and willingness to wait, and forgiveness for every time I get impatient with my own healing.

I try to release the yoke of immediacy, and learn to bear rest. For many of us who live with mental illness, the discomfort of our emotions or thoughts can be too much to bear, and we seek any and all ways to get rid of them. Sometimes we choose a healthy way to step outside ourselves . . . and sometimes we don't. Sometimes we're in such distress that we act out in ways that damage our relationships or friendships, or even hurt ourselves. I am daily trying to learn that my anxiety and depression might not need immediate attention. Tumbling emotions and scattered thoughts might not be providing the most reality-based account of the world around me. I try to trust the poet Rainer Maria Rilke when he said, "Just keep going. No feeling is final." Sometimes I just survive the moment and get out of the grocery store. (This is more common during my anxiety episodes—I can't really achieve mindfulness when my mind is just a fire alarm.) Sometimes—God willing, may there be more of these for all of us—I can step back and ask myself: *What are you trying to get right now? Connection, support, love, affirmation? How can you get that in a way that is kind to you and to others?* Under this newer yoke, I try not to react to every emotion immediately, but to wait and breathe and see what happens when my body returns to rest. If the concern persists, time to attend to it. If it fades, take a note for the next therapy session.

I try to release the yoke of commodified self-care, and learn to bear one step on a longer path. Self-care as a concept has been commercialized to the point of laughability. Our stereotypes are a mud mask with a bubble bath, the secret chocolate hidden in the boring "Bills Paid" file, the gray t-shirt with loopy script proclaiming, "It's wine o'clock everywhere!" Self-care, the cultural story goes, is the little indulgence in the face of desperation, a little bit of naughtiness totally justified by the stressors of life. But self-care, much as the marketers would rather we think otherwise, is not a one-time-use impulse buy or a single stolen moment. Sustainable and restorative self-care is a collection of actions each person can take to support and encourage their own mental, emotional, and physical health. By necessity, this includes the five-minute breaks where we escape from our immediate stressors, but if we stop our self-care there, we miss the lighter burden. Self-care helps us cope in intense moments, but also can create and sustain long-term resilience in the face of recurrent stress.

Determining my own self-care regimen has been a journey of discernment. Of course I wanted to do everything at once, and perfectly the first time, which as it turns out is a good portion of why I burn out and start spiraling into anxiety and depression. Medication has been one of my constants, and thankfully, one of the ones I can do most easily and see the most effect. Without citalopram, my thoughts have a lovely capacity for digging deeper each day, finding new rock bottoms for me to get stuck in. Citalopram gives my emotions a basement. We might stay down there, getting moldy and forgotten in the unlit corners, but we can't go lower, and eventually we get bored and go upstairs. (Most of the time. Some days are still tough.) Breakfast before coffee—now a laminated sticky note stuck to the French press—is another ludicrously simple practice of self-care that keeps my days more balanced. (Keeping it to one mug of coffee helps, too.) Leafy green things seem to be good for my insides and for my soul. (Here I get to cheat and do a two-for-one with a kale smoothie before coffee.) Also on the self-care list are an outdoor walk when I can get it and sunshine through a window when I can't; as the saying goes, I'm basically a houseplant with more complicated emotions.[1] Hot baths are my secret weapon when I'm emotionally wrung out; my record so far is three in one afternoon, in a hotel after a speaking gig, where I was so drained that I watched most of the other speakers on livestream, with my laptop perched on the long sink counter.

But self-care is not limited only to the physical. Restorative and sustaining self-care also involves emotional and mental self-assessment. Where have I gone beyond my own limits? Where am I pushing myself too much? When do I let my mind shut off and rest? Whose presence is comforting and assuring to my heart? This covers all manner of life: work, home, family of origin, partners and children, hobbies and activities, friends, strangers on the internet. Every one of us has energetic limits, and many of us don't come to know them till we've gone way past and are suddenly wondering why the smallest request from our coworker / child / spouse / neighbor / that one high school friend on FB has suddenly filled us with unbridled rage. It is not uncommon for many of us—especially those of us in marginalized or minority communities, who feel extra pressure to "prove" ourselves—to not know when to slow down, or how. Finding my own mental and emotional limits, and planting boundaries a gracious space ahead of them, has taken time, experimentation, and lots of failure. I tend to say a compliant, "Yes" instead of speaking the holy, "No." My wife and I rejoice every time I turn something down, as a positive reinforcement of how important knowing my limits is. I periodically take my email and social media off my phone, or close my direct messages to everyone but trusted friends. I turn off notifications at night. I remind myself that even Paul, "all things to all people," did not get DMs from strangers at three a.m.

Self-care, despite its commodification, is the opposite of a quick fix. It is a lived pattern of long-term small steps to recognize who I am, what I need, and how I can be restored to the wholeness of the God image in which I am made. I've never done it perfectly (much to my chagrin); I've often thought myself to be doing just fine until one morning I realize I've been halfway into my second cup of coffee before I even think about breakfast for two weeks in a row. Usually this realization is closely preceded by, "Why am I so tired and irritable?" and quickly followed by, "*oh for Pete's sake.*" Just because I know better doesn't mean every day I do better. It just means it's quicker to get back on track when I've slipped off.

Self-care, and the boundaries it requires, runs contrary to much of what cultural Christianity might tell us. We are supposed to be one body, endlessly attentive to the needs of the other, giving up our selves just as Jesus gave up himself for all of us. What I've come to believe is that this, too, is the wrong yoke. Teaching that our own needs must come last tells a lie about our bodies, minds, and hearts refuted by the very first story of Scripture—*they need rest.* God, powerful enough to organize every atom, needed a break, and we, made in their image, do too. To act as if I have no boundaries or limits of my own is to take up an old yoke and refuse the newer, lighter one offered. So **I try to release the yoke of savior syndrome, and learn to bear truth**.

The savior of the world, both in biblical story and lived experience, is a wily being. The canonical gospels capture four artistically distinct portraits of the same man; the church's history with him has been, most succinctly said, a bit varied; our own personal experiences with what it means to pray to and walk with a God who has known the feeling of a stubbed toe and a broken heart is rich and diverse. One of the most surprising things about Jesus, for me as a person *and* as a pastor, is that I am apparently not him. According to core Christian tradition, there has been only one savior, and it is not me. Shockingly and rudely, I have not been given the power of instantaneous healing for any stranger I meet along the way. Most of my encounters with people are not a quick prayer and quicker healing as I'm on my way to another village but a long-term relationship, with all the slogs and highs and lows that come with what it means to be human.

I have also, to this day, not met Jesus. (*You know what I mean.*) I have met people who dwell in their bodies as light and compelling as a flame on a candle; people who move through the world with such tenderness and grace that crowds are drawn to them; people who see the truth in things and tell it, smiling wryly, knowing that I don't want to hear it and yet need to. I have even met people whose words and actions have helped in my healing. None of them have been Jesus. It appears there was only one savior, and it is not any of us.

It is burdensome, and heavy in many ways, to recognize that I cannot save anyone, not really. I can move with kindness, and speak with honesty, and cry out against oppression—including pulling a stranger aside to explain, even if I accurately sense I am about to get cussed out, that we do not, under any circumstances, use the r-word as a slur here—and be present to another's pain, but at the end of the day, no one human can be fully responsible for the complete and total salvation of another. It is heavy to say this, because I know how badly some of us want to save another, and I know how badly some of us long to be saved by someone else. But I have also known what it is to be the person others turn to for saving, and I have seen what it did to friends and relationships when I depended on them to save my life. Much as it is heavy to say that none of us are saviors, it is so much heavier to try to pretend to be. I in no way say this to downplay or dismiss the amazing work done by those who are heroic in the face of despair, who have talked someone through a crisis or arrived just in time or kept up phone calls even when they felt like they had nothing helpful to say. We save each other all the time. But none of us can be the *sole* savior for another—the sole source of healing or of hope. Each of us, whether we live with mental illness or not, is stuck with the light-and-heavy burden that we are going to have to participate in saving ourselves, too.

But, of course, that can become a too-heavy yoke too. Many of us with mental illness—maybe a few of you others, too—know what it's like to buy yet another self-help book or try one more thirty-day-regimen-to-better-whatever. I want to fix myself. I want to be better for the people that I love, and happier in my own skin. And while I cannot expect one person to grant all that to me, neither can I create it for myself alone. So each day, **I try to release the yoke of independence, and learn to bear community**. I cannot do everything on my own. Most days I cannot even do it with just me and Jesus. The light burden for me is to know that I need other people—a whole lot of them.

I need people who know me. I have been saved in small ways over and over by friends bold enough to tell me the truth about who I have been and who I am being. I used to think the label of "best friend" was reserved for that tier of people who had seen me at my worst, using every bad coping mechanism to run from any chance at helping myself actually feel better, and still loved me. Today, I wonder if it is not the friends who have seen my ugliness and gone, "Oh, honey, no. Let's not let you do this again." These are people who see me wrapping my hands around the old yoke and gently say, "Didn't you say last year you wanted to try something new?"

I need people who can face pain without trying to fix it. One of the gifts of my life, from high school till now, has been friendships with people who do *not* live with chronic mental illness, and friends who do but have done the work to disconnect their own journey from others'. I have dear friends who model what it looks like to respond to a situation without spinning anxiety or deep despair. In the face of my own struggle, they do not dismiss it or call me "crazy," but hold unanxious and unexpectant space for me to flail around in. They do not try to fix me or swoop in to save me from myself. They simply let me kick against the goads I've chosen until I'm ready (or worn out enough) to try an easier yoke. This is not limited to friends, either; one of my most sustaining communities has been the r/relationships side of Reddit, where strangers discuss anonymous posts and offer (even disagree on) advice. Reading through a multitude of responses to emotional reactions and situations has helped me re-calibrate my internal sense of what is not necessarily "normal" but at least comes closer than my anxious brain likes to be. In that space, everyone knows they cannot fix another person's problems—only offer one voice in a collective of experiences as we try to be kinder and more intentional human beings.

I need professionals. Therapy, career coaches, and social work are complex systems to navigate, and finding the right match—accessible, financially achievable, enjoyable without being too easy on me—takes work. (I have had to learn it is okay to ask for help finding a therapist.) But in working with a licensed and trained professional, I allow myself the help of someone who can tease out the stories behind my cycling thoughts or disruptive habits and then call me into newer ideas—and then be properly compensated for it. The work of walking with someone living with mental illness is unspeakably hard work, and the frustration of figuring out who's in my health insurance and who's got a sliding scale (with the help of friends who like research) paid off in a big way knowing that the person who was helping me is also helped by another system.

I need to be okay with calling the people who can help me when I am very not okay. In my worst times, I can feel how aggressively I want help from those who cannot help me. I want the help of someone I look up to, I want the help of the person who broke my heart, I want to feel seen and validated in my pain by someone whose opinion I have deemed trustworthy. Annoyingly enough, this is not who can actually help, nor who should, when I am in my worst places. Who needs to help me then is someone who can assess my safety and risk, and who can act if I am a danger to myself or others. In accepting the lighter yoke of community, I have learned that I cannot make an unqualified person my emergency call; it risks my own chance of safety and help, and puts an unimaginable burden on them.

I also need people who think I'm okay, even when I'm not. For me, to stay grounded and focused, I need the basic social connections of day-to-day life. The random chats in the office, simple hellos from peers at conferences, the self-checkout associate who doesn't know I'm having a panic attack about the stupid bananas setting off the scanner alert—these small interactions help my mind disconnect from its own worry and despair, and re-engage with the concrete world around me. One of the hardest things, for many of us, during the COVID-19 pandemic was how fraught and sparse our ordinary social interactions became. For me, the simple exchanges of basic social interaction keep me feeling like another human, rather than a ball of anxieties.

I need a healthy way I can help. Participating in the greater hope of others is one of the most important, most human, most divine things I can do. This is not because it can shift my mentally ill brain to "at least you don't have it worse" (although some people do have this reaction and it can be helpful!) but because it is intrinsically a good thing to help others. Our bodies know this; when we help others, our brains release neurotransmitters that boost our mood and reduce stress. Helping others gives us a sense of purpose and connection. Yet the depth of need in the world can feel unnavigable. Finding a way to help without creating a system of reliance (where I, as an individual, am the only source of hope) has been a huge source of both sustainable self-care and increased mental health. (Someone once said the second greatest rule in life is to love your neighbor as yourself. Can't remember who. Sounds wise, though, doesn't it?)

I need me. I love so many people. I rely on so many. And I also have a role to play in letting go of my heavy yoke and grabbing on to something lighter. Even on my hardest days, I need me—shaky, sad, anxious, exhausted—to do just one small thing that I know can help. On my easier days, I need me—happy, creative, generous—to keep up my self-care practices and maintain my boundaries so that I can feel my strength sustained and refilled. I need me to step up for me. I do my best (even when it isn't great).

I also need Jesus. (You probably saw that one coming.) But not because in Jesus the way is perfect or the burden disappears. Not because if I "lay it at the foot of the cross" or "remember it's in God's hands" that suddenly my mental illness is perfectly and eternally cured. I need Jesus because I forget, so often, everything I've said above. I forget to care for myself; I forget to ask for help; I forget to respect my friends' boundaries. I need Jesus because when my unhealthy mind tells me I have absolutely ruined everything, when my heart beats a message that no one can ever love me, I cling with white-knuckled hands to the promise that there is no one unlovable, there is no one irredeemable. Every time I recognize that the bar across my shoulders is the heavy one I was supposed to leave behind, I remember too that each of my days is a fresh start.

This is the promise, the only miracle I know and the best prescription I can offer: The work of living with mental illness can be easier than we make it. We do not have to burden ourselves with bearing it alone; there are therapists, and doctors, and friends, and 24/7 crisis interventionists, and church communities ready to walk with us. We do not have to keep doing what we've always done in the hope of suddenly, against all past performance, doing it better; we can rest, and weep, and after thrashing around a lot, grumpily agree to try something new. We can admit that we are not Jesus: We cannot save ourselves; we need good food and a place to lay our heads; and our pain is not for the saving of the world but a wound that needs holy and careful tending. We will always be carrying something, but beloveds, I believe it can be easier.

QUESTIONS TO ASK

- What heavy yoke are you used to?
- What would a lighter yoke look like?
- What small immediate self-care actions can you take to give your body and mind rest?
- What little good thing did you already do for yourself today?
- What regular self-care habit could you start today?
- When your emotions feel overwhelming, what do you usually want to do?
- What might a more sustainable and compassionate choice (for you and others!) look like?
- How can you remind yourself of that the next time you feel overwhelmed?
- Who are the people that you need?

ACKNOWLEDGMENTS

This book was crowbarred out of my heart page by page during the COVID-19 pandemic. First and last, my gratitude goes to the medical professionals who cared for so many, the politicians who acted to protect their people, the restaurant owners and food service staff who put up signs for curbside pickup, the parents and guardians who struggled to keep their children's joy in the midst of fear, the teachers and school staff who drained their own emotional wells to keep their students' learning buoyant, every person in frontline work who found their lives devalued even as their jobs became essential—to every person who took an incredible crisis in our world seriously that we might preserve the lives of others. Your caution and care is the reason we made it to today. We will never know how many lives you saved, and we will never be able to thank you enough.

More than twenty years in and out of therapy means that I cannot name every doctor and therapist who has walked with me along the way. Know that your work bears fruit in ways that can never be fully named.

So many friends have helped in lifting the burden of mental illness. I'm especially grateful to my high school friends Mandy and Missy, who loved and preserved our friendship even as I struggled to be myself; to fellow perfectionists like Natalia and Laura Jean who know too well how we make our own journeys harder, but can make me laugh about it; to Dianna, Anna, Ryan, Austen, and Ari, for composing a D&D campaign slash trivia team that brings fresh joy every week; and always to the nine women who accompanied me through seminary and into our diverse calls today: Ali, Ashley, Gretchen, Hannah, Jamie, Jill, Kim, Michelle, and last but not least Lisa, who sends the very gentlest of reminder emails when I miss a deadline.

As always, thank you, Mom. You wove protection around me as a teenager so that I might make it safely to self-understanding and growth.

And for forever, my beautiful and brilliant Michelle, this book is for you. You live with such fierce kindness in the face of my journey, and call me ever to the deeper joy within me and within our life together. You, of all people, make my burden lighter.

NOTES

PREFACE

1. Mark 5:21–43; Matthew 9:18–26; Luke 8:40–56.

CHAPTER ONE: SIN

1. My parishioner Douglas says, "Do you think Jesus was a *good* carpenter, or do you think when he set out to do ministry that everyone nodded and said, 'Yeah, tables just aren't for you, my dude'?"
2. In the stories in Mark 1:24; Luke 4:34; Matthew 8:29–31; Mark 5:7–9; and Luke 8:28–30.
3. In Mark's version of the Gerasene demoniac, the possessed man "bruises himself with stones."
4. Organisation for Economic Co-operation and Development, "Employment: Time Spent in Paid and Unpaid Work, by Sex," last updated February 2021, https://stats.oecd.org/index.aspx?queryid=54757.
5. Misty Heggeness, "Estimating the Immediate Impact of the COVID-19 Shock on Parental Attachment to the Labor Market and the Double Bind of Mothers," *Review of Economics of the Household* 18, no. 4 (October 2020), 1–26.
6. Caroline Criado Perez, *Invisible Women: Exposing Data Bias in a World Designed for Men* (New York: Harry N. Abrams, 2019), 186.
7. Henna Budhwani, Kristine Ria Hearld, and Daniel Chavez-Yenter, "Depression in Racial and Ethnic Minorities: The Impact

of Nativity and Discrimination," *Racial Ethnic Health Dispari-ties* 2, no. 1 (2015), 34–42.

8. Centers for Disease Control and Prevention, "Summary Health Statistics: National Health Interview Survey: 2018. Table A-7," https://www.cdc.gov/nchs/nhis/shs/tables.htm.

9. Nagy A. Youssef et al., "The Effects of Trauma, with or without PTSD, on the Transgenerational DNA Methylation Alterations in Human Offsprings," *Brain Sciences* 8, no. 5 (May 2018), 83.

10. *American Psychiatric Association*, "Mental Health Disparities: Diverse Populations" (2017).

11. "Mental Health Disparities: Diverse Populations."

12. Substance Abuse and Mental Health Services Administration, *Racial/Ethnic Differences in Mental Health Service Use among Adults*, HHS Publication No. SMA-15-4906 (Rockville, MD: Substance Abuse and Mental Health Services Administration, 2015).

13. From the Black hymn "Lift Every Voice and Sing."

14. Margaret O. Akinhanmi et al., "Racial Disparities in Bipolar Disorder Treatment and Research: a Call to Action," *Bipolar Disorders* 20, no. 6 (2018), 506–14.

15. Michelle S. Goeree, John C. Ham, and Daniela Iorio, "Race, Social Class, and Bulimia Nervosa," IZA Discussion Paper No. 5823, available at SSRN, https://ssrn.com/abstract=1877636.

CHAPTER TWO: PRAYER

1. Peter Boelens et al., "The Effect of Prayer on Depression and Anxiety: Maintenancle of Positive Influence One Year after Prayer Intervention," *International Journal of Psychiatry in Medicine 43, no. 1* (March 22, 2012), 85–98.

2. Kanita Dervic et al., "Religious Affiliation and Suicide Attempt," *American Journal of Psychiatry* 161, no. 12 (December 1, 24), 2303–08.

3. Megan C. Lytle et al., "Association of Religiosity With Sexual Minority Suicide Ideation and Attempt," *American Journal of Preventative Medicine 54, no. 5* (March 14, 2018), 644–51.

4. Luke 18:9–14.

5. Luke 19:1–10.
6. Matthew 12:43–45.

CHAPTER THREE: SEEKING TREATMENT

1. Mark 5:1–7.
2. Felicitas Goodman, *The Exorcism of Anneliese Michel* (Eugene, Oregon: Resource Publications, 25).
3. Gospel of John, chapters 9–11.
4. Job 40:1–5.
5. Luke 9:23: "Take up your cross and follow me."
6. Jesus is unable to accomplish many healings in his hometown (Mark 6:5) and also takes two tries to heal a blind man (Mark 8:22–25).
7. The paralytic at Capernaum (Matthew 9:1–8, Mark 2:1–12, Luke 5:17–26) and the paralytic at Bethesda (John 5:1–18).
8. Luke 13:10–17.
9. Exorcism: Matthew 12:22–32 and Luke 11:14–23; also in Matthew 9:32–34. Healing: Mark 7:31–37; Mark 8:22–26; Bartimaeus in Matthew 20:29–34, Mark 10:46–52, and Luke 18:35–43; and John 9:1–12.
10. C.S. Lewis, *Voyage of the Dawn Treader* (London: Geoffrey Bles, 1952).

CHAPTER FOUR: SADNESS

1. Center for Behavioral Health Statistics and Quality (CBHSQ), Substance Abuse and Mental Health Services Administration (SAMHSA), U.S. Department of Health and Human Services (HHS), and RTI International, *Results from the 2017 National Survey on Drug Use and Health*, https://www.samhsa.gov/data/sites/default/files/cbhsq-reports/NSDUHDetailedTabs2017/NSDUHDetailedTabs2017.htm. (As we recover from the COVID-19 pandemic, I have no doubt this number will significantly jump for at least the next year or two.)
2. Psalm 30:5.
3. Julia Raifman et al., "Association of State Laws Permitting Denial of Services to Same-Sex Couples With Mental Distress in Sexual

Minority Adults: A Difference-in-Difference-in-Differences Analysis," *JAMA Psychiatry* 75, no. 7 (2018), 671–677, doi:10.11/jamapsychiatry.2018.0757.
4. Author's note to editor: Sorry, Lisa.
5. Ruth 1:3–5 and 1:19–20.
6. Ruth 4:17.
7. 1 Samuel 1:2 and 1:6.
8. 1 Samuel 1:8.
9. 1 Samuel 1:9–18.
10. Psalm 6:7, 13:2, 25:16, 38:11, 31:12, and 44:15.
11. Psalm 22:1.
12. Psalm 42:5–6, 11, and 43:5.

CHAPTER FIVE: WORRY

1. This is her real name and she is one of my favorite people.
2. 1 Timothy 2:9.
3. Luke 10:40–42; John 11:32–35.
4. Esther 4:1–14.
5. Joshua 1:9; Isaiah 35:4, Isaiah 41:10, Isaiah 43:1; Psalm 23:4; Mark 4:39–40; John 14:1; Revelation 1:17.

CHAPTER SIX: PSYCHOSIS

1. Ironically, I was never told that my MMPI indicated I had depression or social anxiety, but I *was* told I had a score on the high range of normal in the Lie factor, meaning I want people to think I'm morally better than I actually am. I looked at the assessor, who seemed expectant that I would argue against this, and simply said, ". . . don't most pastors?"
2. Because of the stigma associated with the phrase "psychotic episodes," in this chapter I will primarily use "experiences of psychosis."
3. Exodus 3:1–12.
4. Exodus 4:27; Exodus 4:30–31; Exodus 7:14–12:32.
5. 1 Samuel 3:1.
6. 1 Samuel 8:10.

7. 1 Samuel 9:17 and 10:10–13.
8. 1 Samuel 16:11–13 and 14–23.
9. 1 Samuel 7:1–17 and 12:1–15.
10. 1 Kings 19:13; Isaiah 6.2–3, Ezekiel 3:3.
11. Jeremiah 13:1–11 and 27–28.
12. 1 Corinthians 14:29.

CHAPTER SEVEN: TRAUMA

1. Walter Wink, *Jesus and Nonviolence: A Third Way* (Minneapolis: Fortress Press, 23); also in Matthew, Sheila, and Dennis Linn's *Don't Forgive Too Soon: Extending the Two Hands That Heal* (Paulist Press, 1997).
2. Genesis 50:20.
3. Deuteronomy 23:1.
4. Isaiah 56:3–5; "never cut off" is very likely a turn of phrase on the "cutting off" of castration.
5. Matthew 18:15–22 and Luke 17:5–6.
6. Matthew 5:27–30; John 7:53–8:11.
7. James Cone, *The Cross and the Lynching Tree (Orbis, September 1, 2011)*.
8. National Center for Injury Prevention and Control, Division of Violence Prevention, "Preventing Child Abuse & Neglect," last updated April 2020, https://www.cdc.gov/violenceprevention/childabuseandneglect/fastfact.html.
9. Ibid, "Preventing Intimate Partner Violence," last updated October 2020, https://www.cdc.gov/violenceprevention/intimate partnerviolence/fastfact.html.
10. Ibid, "Sexual Violence Is Preventable," last updated December 2020, https://www.cdc.gov/injury/features/sexual-violence/index.html.
11. On average, it takes a survivor seven attempts to leave for good.
12. Deuteronomy 22:28–29.

CHAPTER EIGHT: FOOD

1. Strategic Training Initiative for the Prevention of Eating Disorders (STRIPED) and the Academy for Eating Disorders, "The Social and Economic Cost of Eating Disorders in the United States of America," June 2020, https://www.hsph.harvard.edu/striped/report-economic-costs-of-eating-disorders/.
2. Mary Pipher, 1994.
3. Millie Plotkin, "Eating Disorders by the Numbers," *Families Empowered and Supporting Treatment of Eating Disorders*, August 2020, https://www.feast-ed.org/eating-disorders-by-the-numbers/.
4. Plotkin, "Eating Disorders by the Numbers."
5. Mark 1:9–13; Matthew 3:13–4:11; Luke 3:21–4:13.
6. Deuteronomy 8:3.
7. 1 Kings 19:1–8.
8. Exodus 16:1–21.
9. Isaiah 25:6, 55:1.
10. Isaiah 55:2, 57:5, and 58:3–6.

CHAPTER NINE: ADDICTION

1. Leviticus 10:9.
2. Genesis 19:30–38 and 2 Samuel 11:13.
3. Proverbs 20:1, 21:17, 23:20–21, and 23:29–35.
4. Isaiah 5:11–12, 5:22; and Habakkuk 2:15–17.
5. Isaiah 28:7–8, Jeremiah 25:27, and Ezekiel 23:31–34.
6. For church membership: Romans 13:13, Galatians 5:19–21, 1 Corinthians 5:11 and 6:10, Ephesians 5:18, and 1 Peter 4:3–4. For leaders: 1 Timothy 3:2–3, 8; and Titus 1:7, 2:3.
7. 1 Corinthians 11:23–26; 1 Timothy 5:23.
8. Ecclesiastes 2:24, 3:13, 5:18, 8:15, and 9:7. It is to Ecclesiastes that the phrase "eat, drink, and be merry" is attributed, but it does not occur in that exact phrasing in the actual text.
9. Psalm 104:15.
10. Isaiah 55:1.
11. John 2:1–11.
12. Matthew 11:18–19 and Luke 7:33–35.

13. "4. Made a searching and fearless moral inventory of ourselves. 5. Admitted to God, to ourselves, and to another human being the exact nature of our wrongs. 6. Were entirely ready to have God remove all these defects of character. 7. Humbly asked God to remove our shortcomings. 8. Made a list of all persons we had harmed, and became willing to make amends to them all. 9. Made direct amends to such people wherever possible, except when to do so would injure them or others."

CHAPTER TEN: SUICIDE

1. Al-Anon is a companion program to Alcoholics Anonymous, specifically designed for family, friends, and loved ones of those who struggle with addiction.
2. *Suicidal ideation*: thinking about or planning suicide. This encompasses a wide range, from a fleeting thought to a concrete plan, and many places in between.
3. If you're feeling right now like I was feeling on that bathroom floor, please look at the resources at the end of this chapter.
4. Abimelech in Judges 9:53; Saul and his armor-bearer in 1 Samuel 31; Ahithophel in 2 Samuel 17:23; and King Zimri in 1 Kings 16:15–20.
5. Judges 16.
6. Acts 16.
7. Matthew 27:1–10.
8. Acts 1:18. Acts is considered by many scholars to be written by the same author as the Gospel of Luke, which may be why it tells a different story than the Gospel according to Matthew.
9. Jonah 4:9–10.
10. Philippians 1:23.
11. Job 3:3.
12. Psalm 6:6; Psalm 13:2; Psalm 22:6.
13. Caitlin Ryan et al., "Family Acceptance in Adolescence and the Health of LGBT Young Adults," *Journal of Child and Adolescent Psychiatric Nursing* 23, no. 4 (November 2010), 205–13.

14. Stanford Graduate School of Business, "No-fault Divorce Laws May Have Improved Women's Well-being," Newswise, June 24.

CHAPTER ELEVEN: BOUNDARIES

1. Matthew 25:31–46.
2. Matthew 25:14–30.
3. Matthew 25:1–13.
4. If you haven't had this happen and don't know someone who has had this happen, just consider yourself lucky.
5. Statistics from the Faith Communities Today 2010 national survey of 11,000 American congregations.
6. Matthew 18:1–9.
7. Matthew 18:15–20.
8. Matthew 18:21–35.

CHAPTER TWELVE: SELF-CARE

1. Originally seen in Reza Farazmand's webcomic Poorly Drawn Lines.